Dartmoor and South Devon

Brian Knapp

Illustrations by Duncan McCrae and Brian Knapp

London
GEORGE ALLEN & UNWIN
Boston   Sydney

George Allen & Unwin (Publishers) Ltd,
40 Museum Street, London WC1A 1LU, UK

George Allen & Unwin (Publishers) Ltd,
Park Lane, Hemel Hempstead, Herts HP2 4TE, UK

Allen & Unwin Inc.,
9 Winchester Terrace, Winchester, Mass 01890, USA

George Allen & Unwin Australia Pty Ltd,
8 Napier Street, North Sydney, NSW 2060, Australia

First published in 1984

ISSN 0265–3117

Sketch-maps on pp. 31, 34, 36, 42, 43, 52, 58 and 69 based in part on
Ordnance Survey mapping: Crown Copyright reserved.

British Library Cataloguing in Publication Data

Knapp, Brian
   Dartmoor and South Devon. – (Unwin
countryside guides; 2)
1. Devon – Description and travel –
Guide-books
I. Title
914.23′5   DA670.D5
ISBN 0–04–551082–2 ╱

Set in 9 on 10 point Palatino by Nene Phototypesetters, Northampton
and printed in Hong Kong by Colorcraft Ltd

Contents

Introduction: getting away from it all

South Devon is one of Britain's most popular holiday areas. Trips to the seaside began in the 18th century when a certain Dr Russell published a book called 'On glandular consumption and the use of sea water in diseases of the glands'. At this time, resorts were no more than places where health could be restored: very little thought was given to the beautiful surrounding countryside. However, by the 19th century, holidays provided a means of escape from the pollution of cities and enabled people to rediscover the natural world. Spurred on by the entrepreneurs of the Great Western Railway, by the desire to find wide sandy beaches and to secure the best chance of fine weather, people began to discover the richness of South Devon. Today, holiday-makers from all over Europe enjoy the variety of the landscape, which includes sandy beaches for a lazy day, cliff-tops for a leisurely walk, and moorland for a sense of 'the great outdoors'. Despite the great influx of visitors, South Devon seems able to contain them all. True, the main roads are congested at the height of summer, but everyone is free to leave their cars and venture just a few steps on to the cliff-top or stroll up to a granite tor. In this guide, you will find routes that will help you to understand a little better how the South Devon countryside has evolved and so increase your enjoyment of a wonderful part of Britain as you get away from it all.

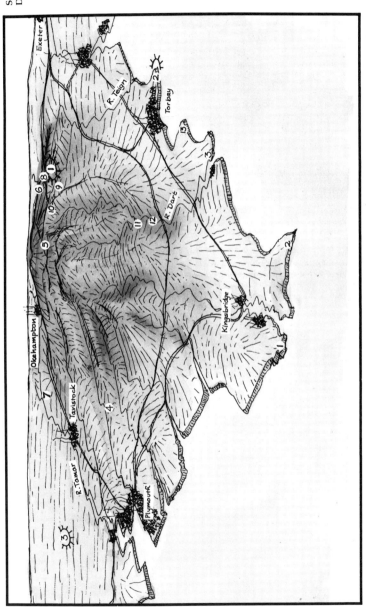

Exeter

R. Teign

Torbay

6 8 1
10 9
5

11 12

R. Dart

13

3

Okehampton

Tavistock

R. Tamar

7

4

Plymouth

Kingsbridge

2

2

ASH

(50–80 ft; 15–25 m)

One of the tallest of Britain's trees, the ash is readily distinguished in summer by its large leaves, up to 12 in (30 cm) long, which are made up of five pairs of leaflets. In winter its twigs have a prominent black terminal bud. The ash is one of the hungriest broadleaved trees, taking many of the nutrients from the soil on which it grows and starving plants that try to survive beneath it. Ash trees are found particularly on north and east sides of hills, provided the soil is free draining. They have interesting single-winged 'keys' whose twisted form causes them to spin as they fall in such a way that the seed end always reaches the ground first. Ash has been widely coppiced for poles and handles.

PART 1   BACKGROUND

The countryside as it was

In the beginning

We tend to think of the land beneath our feet as everlasting, but some 500 million years ago South Devon simply did not exist. Where sun-bathers now lie on the beaches of Torbay, and walkers tramp across the wilderness of Dartmoor, there was nothing but a vast warm sea. To the south lay a large continent on which no plant flowered or animal walked, for at this early time life was still confined to the sea. Over a thousand miles to the north lay another great continent, which was slowly moving southwards on a collision course, crushing and tearing the rocks of the sea bed and squeezing them up into towering mountains higher than the Himalayas of today. These mountains stretched across what became Ireland, Wales, northern England and Scotland. Although South Devon remained under the sea and was largely unscathed by the period of mountain building, as the mountains grew, so torrential rivers began to rush down their flanks. The river waters washed boulders, sands and muds into the sea, building vast deltas just as material carried by the Mississippi builds into deltas in the Gulf of Mexico today. Wherever the sands accumulated near this ancient coast, their ever increasing weight turned them into a rock: called sandstone. The muds were carried away from the coast, settling out on the sea floor and building layer upon layer. Eventually the water was squeezed out and the muds turned into a rock called shale. Shales and sandstones are some of Devon's most common rocks and the deep red, iron-stained deposits are a distinctive part of the landscape. In fact, so well are these ancient rocks displayed in Devon that a whole part of geological history has been named the Devonian period.

As millions of years passed, the northern mountains were slowly worn down by the weather until they were reduced first to hills and then to low plains. The once torrential rivers gradually became more and more sluggish until they were able to carry only the finest muds out to sea. However, between the places where rivers muddied the coastal waters, the sea remained clear and in its warm, shallow waters flourished great reefs of corals. One of the largest stretches lay between what are now Plymouth and Torquay, a 'Great Barrier Reef' that was later to be formed into the dove-grey limestone rocks common in the cliffs of the area today.

All was not, however, quiet in these Devonian seas. From time to time there were tremendous earthquakes, and underwater volcanoes punched up through the sea bed, their eruptions sending plumes of gas and ash towering into the sky. At the same time, great tongues of lava spilled out, covering the reefs and killing the coral. Yet although corals were destroyed time after time by lava, on each occasion they recolonised the lava and grew again, so that today limestone and lava occur side by side in the cliffs along the coast.

(Opposite) **Okehampton 500 million years ago**

Some 300 million years ago, the sea bed had become very shallow and conditions on land were also slowly changing. Where once there had been no life, there were now forests of giant ferns, living near the coast in swamps; from time to time the sea rose and drowned the swamps, smothering the ferns in layers of sea-borne mud. Slowly the ferns decayed in the mud, producing a form of coal that Devon men call culm. In Devon the coals were only thin, but in northern England at this time, great coal seams were being formed, which eventually provided the basis for the Industrial Revolution.

By this time, mud, silt and sand had been accumulating for hundreds of millions of years, occasionally laced with outpourings from volcanoes. However, although a mass of rocks had been formed, they all remained below the sea. Now it was time to make them into land, for the continents were once again on the move.

For over a hundred million years the old ocean had been growing smaller and smaller; now it was disappearing completely, squeezed between the irresistible force of the jaws of two continents, moving slowly from the south and from the north. The 'crunch' was mighty and long. The ocean bed was crushed and torn, its rocks jolted and jostled; the muds and sands folded into tightly contorted forms and sometimes even baked so that their solid minerals changed into completely new forms.

The traumatic events lasted more than 50 million years and wrought some profound changes deep within the Earth's crust. Many of the shales, for example, were put under sufficient pressure to turn them into slates. Tens of kilometres below the surface, great splits opened within the crust through which plumes of molten rock rose, melting everything in their paths. By about 270 million years ago these vast balloon-shaped masses of molten rock had risen beneath Devon and Cornwall, slowly 'eating' their way ever higher until they finally cooled and turned into solid granite: the heart of Dartmoor had been formed. By the time they finally came to rest, the rising granites had arched up and baked the overlying rocks. In so doing, they had provided the mineral riches that were later to be the foundation of Devon's mining industry.

Molten rock from the Earth's interior is like a witch's cauldron rich in ingredients. Some parts of the mixture are very runny and can rise up far into the overlying rock, following natural cracks and fissures. As these materials rise and move away from the source of heat, they become cooler and change from liquid to solid, slowly filling in the cracks through which they have flowed. Some materials, such as compounds of tin, can only remain liquid at extremely high temperatures, whereas others, such as iron, lead and copper, travel upwards much further before they become solid. The result is the world's largest chemicals factory – a natural way of separating metals vertically one above the other. Thus, when the granite finally began to cool (and its deepest parts have not completely cooled even today!), it had provided Devon not only with one of Britain's toughest rocks, but also with some of its richest mineral veins. This was also the time

(Opposite) **Torbay 350 million years ago**

when boiling water, released from within the granite, began the intense weathering of the granite margin, and contributed to the formation of the famous china clay whose mining leaves such distinctive white moonscapes.

When the granite was formed, it was still deep within a mountain range, thousands of feet underground. But, as the mountains were attacked by elements of the weather, they were slowly worn down – destroyed pebble by pebble, grain by grain, in a process that may have lasted 200 million years. As layer after layer of rock was eroded away, slowly the granite came closer and closer to the surface; yet even when the mountains had been reduced to plains, still the granite remained buried. Hundreds of miles to the south, new movements of the Earth were creating the Alps. Devon was far from this turmoil, but the Earth's movements still managed to break the brittle, old rocks of south-west England into pieces, thrusting part up to form Devon and Cornwall while causing other parts to slide and form the English Channel.

Only at this relatively late stage was the granite exposed at the surface, although from this time onwards rain water was able to soak into the cracks in the rock and begin the long process of weathering. Cracks in the granite were common in many places and sparse in others. The granite with massive blocks and few cracks has been better able to resist attack by the weather and now makes hills crowned by the famous tors. These contrast with the areas where intense cracking allowed rain to erode the rock more rapidly, forming the intervening valleys.

The land did not rise smoothly; rather, during the past 50 million years it has been lifted up in a number of jerks, separated by longer periods without movement. Each of the quiet periods gave the sea sufficient time to wear back the land many miles. Today, the landscape of South Devon looks like a grand staircase. The highest tread is formed from granite, then there is a step down to a level of about 1000 ft (300 m), another to about 750 ft (230 m), then another to 430 ft (130 m), and finally a step whose tread now forms most of the cliff-tops at 240 ft (73 m). At the present time, following yet another upward jerk, the sea is cutting back into the land once more. So far it has merely produced wide rocky ledges, which are exposed at low tide. If, however, it is given long enough, it will produce yet one more step to add further variety to the landscape.

The effects of the rising land were not confined just to the coast. With each new rise of land, rivers bit deeply into the surface, carving deep, steep-sided valleys to reach the sea. However, rivers do not work as quickly as the sea and they have insufficient time to do more than divide up each wave-cut step into blocks, in a process of dissection that has made road-building so difficult in Devon.

(Opposite) **Plymouth 250 million years ago**

Totnes in the Ice Age 20000 years ago

The age of ice

We can only hint at what the area was like aeons ago. The rocks we see lying twisted and torn in a cliff provide no more than tantalising glimpses of a period when Devon was at the heart of a mountain range. The top of the cliff, cut off as cleanly as with a knife, tells more clearly of the time when land was lifted up out of the clutches of the sea. However, there is a more recent event which has, somewhat surprisingly, left its mark only in very subtle ways.

About two million years ago – a mere moment in the history of South Devon – the hills and moors were covered with deep soil and thickly mantled in forest. Then something very dramatic happened: within a few hundred years the climate became much cooler and the forest died – Devon had entered the Ice Age.

Away to the north, the mountains of Scotland, northern England and Wales were no longer snow-free in summer, but remained snow-clad throughout the year, accumulating snow on snow until it became compressed into ice. These ice sheets eventually spilled out over lowland England, each year spreading closer to Devon. At the same time as the ice surged forward, the seas shrank back, so that although in Devon rivers still flowed each summer as the winter snow

(Opposite) **The Kingsbridge estuary at Salcombe is so new that a cliff has not yet been formed where the valley sides meet the sea (Walk 1)**

temporarily melted away, they had to flow to a sea many tens of miles off the present coast of Cornwall. As a result they cut channels deep into what had only recently been the sea bed. Cliffs, once sharp and neatly trimmed by the lapping waves, were exposed to the harsh, frosty weather. As ice formed in cracks in the rocks, even the toughest cliffs were sundered and inexorably reduced to rubble. Some, like the platy shales, were more effectively riven by frost than others, producing the heaps of tiny rock slivers that mantle the cliff-foot beaches.

Inland, with the anchoring vegetation long dead, soil slid quickly down to the valleys and bare rock was exposed to the cold. Even the tough granites of the moors could not withstand thousands of years of this frosty climate, and frost-riven debris (called clitter) began to litter the slopes, laying bare the tumble of hill-top blocks that make the famous Dartmoor tors.

Glaciers departed from northern Britain and a more mild climate returned less than 12 000 years ago. On the softer rocks, soil has formed again, trees have grown and the countryside is once more rounded and gentle; but it is a countryside with a very complex and fascinating history.

SILVER BIRCH (80 ft; 25 m)

This graceful tree is both fast growing and short lived. It will tolerate a wide variety of soils and will survive in the most rigorous climates. It is most easily distinguished by its silver-grey scored bark and small toothed leaves. Because of its short life, the silver birch never makes a dominant forest form.

The countryside today

South Devon has taken over 400 million years to form. It has been lifted from the sea many times by forces deep within the Earth, and each time lowered again by the ceaseless erosion of frost, rain and rivers. By chance we see it soon after a very dramatic period when the Ice Age locked up water on land, causing the sea level to fall and enabling rivers in South Devon to form deep valleys. It is only a few thousand years since the ice melted and the sea drowned the valleys. In time, waves will cut cliffs in these valley sides and the estuaries will be filled by material brought down by rivers: the Erme estuary near Kingsbridge is already a wide expanse of sand banks at low tide; others will follow. Tors remain bare and exposed, but at their feet the frost-riven slopes are now mostly weathered into soil and covered with vegetation. In a few tens of thousands of years – scarcely an instant in geological time – all traces of the effects of the Ice Age will have disappeared.

Despite its varied history, the broad landscape of South Devon is quite simple to understand. At its heart lies the great circular granite moorland rising to nearly 2000 ft (about 600 m) above the sea. The granite stands apart from all the other rocks. These, once formed in layers in ancient seas, have been stood on edge by forces within the Earth so that they now appear as near-vertical bands in the cliffs and can be traced from west to east across the whole region, the toughest standing proud as headlands, the weaker being eroded into bays.

With such varied rocks, the even height of the cliff-tops and inland hills is all the more striking, recalling the erosive power of a succession of earlier seas each of which cut across the land as it was raised periodically to its present height. Indeed it is the combination of level plateaux and deeply cut valleys that gives South Devon its distinctive landscape.

And then came man

During the Ice Age, when the northern parts of Britain were held tightly in the grip of ice, conditions in South Devon remained just tolerable enough for early man to survive. In places such as Kent's Cavern (Torquay), he must have fought with hyenas and bears for possession of the shelter provided by the limestone caves. However, he was only holding on in this barren land by the skin of his teeth. Not until the Ice Age faded away and the climate warmed once more were people able to recolonise the countryside.

When Stone Age man ventured across South Devon in the wake of the Ice Age, the countryside was not as it is today. Instead, the lowland moors were covered with trees – oak, ash, beech and elm – which stretched from the valley bottoms to the highest tors. So, like his contemporaries elsewhere in Britain, Stone Age man shunned the densely wooded and marshy valley bottoms and headed for the hills, where trees were less massive and more easily chopped down. We know that early man lived on the moors for centuries, for there are

many oval mounds scattered across the moors which mark the places where chieftains of ancient times were buried. These primitive peoples were able to survive because, paradoxical as it may seem, the climate was warmer and drier soon after the end of the Ice Age than it is today. Unfortunately, at that time nobody gave a thought to the consequences of tree clearance and cultivation on the thin, fragile, moorland soils. They did not know (as soil scientists now tell us) that nutrients are taken up by plants and returned again when they die. They did not realise that, when this cycle is broken by taking plants away for food, the soil can become infertile for ever. They did, however, recognise the fact that, because the soil became useless for crops after a few years, they were continually forced to clear fresh ground. In this way, by accident rather than by design, the upper forests were slowly cleared. With the nutrients now washed away or used up by the crops, and with domestic animals grazing the land, the oak and elm forests could not regenerate in the abandoned sites and the vegetation changed for ever. Today there are only three places where ancient forests survive: Wistman's Wood, Black Tor Beare and Piles Copse. Here the stunted, gnarled oaks hung with green lichens are reminders of the early forests.

Dartmoor was one of the most intensively settled parts of Britain. There are clear signs of 'villages' enclosed by walls, for example at Grimspound (Walk 10), and religious circles and small family plots of cultivated land. Most of the people who settled here arrived from France or the Mediterranean, the first of a long line of invaders whom we now call Celts or ancient Britons. With them they brought a wide variety of skills, including the important techniques of making bronze and iron.

By the time the Iron Age people were landing their boats on the shores of Torbay and moving inland in search of a place to live and farm, there were still many tribes living on the moors. However, by 500 BC the climate was already worsening and the Iron Age people tended to avoid the more exposed sites. Instead they preferred more sheltered locations at the moor edge, and they used the high land only for the forts to which they retreated in time of attack. Thus, although Prestonbury Hill overlooking the Teign valley (Walk 6) has a fine Iron Age fort, there is no evidence of nearby cultivation, whereas forts are even located on lowland coastal sites such as Berry Head (Walk 13). These people included a powerful tribe, the Dumnouii, from whom the county of Devon takes its name.

The Romans did little to alter this pattern of settlement. Their main area of influence in Britain never reached further west than Exeter where, at the end of the Fosse Way, they built a large fort. Beyond this they made little impact on the rural landscape. Nevertheless, Devon was a turbulent region for, despite its firm grip over much of Europe, the Roman Empire was continually under attack on its flanks, and the marauding tribes from northern Europe were eager to gain the prize of new land; a toehold on the South Devon coast would have pro-

(Opposite) **Hay Tor – its massive form exposed by the Ice Age and the slopes at its foot littered with frost-riven debris (View 1)**

vided them with a stronghold from which they would not easily have been displaced. So the Romans built a network of roads from their main base at Exeter westwards to the Tamar and southwards through Totnes towards the coast, building fortified signal stations on the most prominent headlands. At Berry Head they even built a signal station inside a former Iron Age fort. At these places, each within sight of one another, they were able to light a beacon to warn of impending attack. Yet time and events were not on the side of the Romans, and they were eventually forced to abandon the British for ever.

The Saxons arrived in South Devon in the 7th century, some 200 years after their conquests in the east. But they were not, contrary to popular belief, in search of land to burn, houses to pillage and women to rape; they were a true folk movement simply looking for new land to settle. There were some battles, as small groups of Celts defended their territory, but in general there was plenty of room for all and the two peoples quite soon settled down together. After all, their most important task was to grow sufficient food to keep alive and they needed all their time to clear the ground in the densely wooded valleys.

You can get a vivid impression of the country of the Celts and the Saxons by looking at the hamlet, village and hill names on the Ordnance Survey maps. The Saxons largely began our village heritage. These people were firmly based in small hamlets and home-steads sited in clearings hacked out of the valley woodland. The farmers named their clearings 'Fred's clearing in the wood' or 'Charlie's place by the river'. Thus, Lustleigh is Saxon for 'Leofgiest's glade' and Brixham means 'Beorhstige's place'. At the same time they were very interested in the land around and they often named settle-ments, rivers and hills in graphic terms. For example, Ashburton is Saxon for 'a place by the river where ash trees grew', Buckfast means 'stronghold of the deer', and Buckfastleigh is 'forest of Buckfast (village)'. (A more complete list can be found later.)

With such hard work involved in clearing the land, and the acute awareness of the limitations imposed by climate and landscape, each farm, hamlet or village site was chosen with the utmost care. Some people chose riverside locations if enough dry land could be found; others chose sites where valley-side springs emerged, a few chose a fording point; and one or two even chose a sheltered spot near the coast (although most landing places and ports were well up river valleys, for example Totnes and Exeter). The Saxons mainly con-centrated on developing cultivable land such as the lowland plateau south of Dartmoor, leaving the pastoral farming on the moor edge, for the time being at least, in the hands of the Celts.

Life was not easy for these new settlers but, by the time of the Norman Conquest, much land had been cleared and a thriving com-munity established. The Normans did little to alter this pattern, the main change to the countryside being the establishment of a network of castles: medieval 'police stations' designed to keep control over a difficult landscape. At this time, Exeter, by far the largest town, con-tained only 1500 people, and the next largest – Lydford (now only a

The early Saxon settlers in South Devon were much more conscious of, and constrained by, their surroundings than we are today. Hardly surprising, therefore, that they named their settlements after the character of the places where they lived. See how appropriate these names are as you follow the walks and drives in this guide. To help you, the origins of the most common words are given below. Many names are made of two parts, one part being the description of the area and the other someone's name (e.g. Brixham: *brix* a corrupted form of Beorhstige (the person), *ham* a farmstead; hence Brixham means 'the farm or place belonging to Beorhstige').

barton an arable farm (e.g. Rushford Barton)

beare, bere a wood (e.g. Bearscombe near Halwell)

berry a hill (e.g. Berry Head)

brent steep (e.g. Brent Tor near Lydford)

bridge crossing point (e.g. Postbridge)

bury a fort (e.g. Prestonbury Hill, Teign valley)

cleave a cliff (e.g. Lustleigh Cleave)

combe a valley (e.g. Challacombe)

cot, cote an outlying farm of the moor edge (e.g. Middlecott, Chagford)

cut a track formed by cutting away peat to reveal firm ground below (e.g. Cut Hill)

don, down a hill (e.g. Mardon Down)

ford a crossing point (e.g. Chagford)

ham a hamlet (e.g. Brixham)

leigh, ley a wood or clearing (e.g. Buckfastleigh)

ness a headland (e.g. Totnes)

stock, stoc a monastery (e.g. Tavistock)

stow a holy place (e.g. Bridestowe)

ton a hamlet (e.g. Ashburton)

tor a hill (e.g. Hay Tor)

week, wick a stock farm (e.g. East Week)

worthy a farm within the moor (e.g. Willsworthy)

yeo running water (e.g. River Yeo)

Some others not so easy to sort out:

Holne holly

Moretonhampstead moor farm

Princetown site given by Prince of Wales

Shaugh Prior a place in a copse

Widecombe willow valley

hamlet) and Totnes – held a mere 300 each; and these were only distinguishable from farming villages because they were mainly engaged in trade. On the coast no town had been established, and neither Plymouth nor Dartmouth existed. Inland, from a moorside vantage point, the view was over almost continuous tree-tops, only thin wisps of smoking chimneys picking out the villages in their small clearings. But, as the Middle Ages came and the population began to rise, so new land was taken from the forest and moor edge. Unlike much of the rest of England, where large communal fields were the rule, the land was enclosed by thick earth and stone walls, giving Devon one of the most distinctive elements of its countryside.

In the three centuries after the Norman Conquest, the population virtually trebled and trade became more important. In the 12th and 13th centuries, lords of the manor tried to capture some of the trade by setting up town sites on their land in a medieval form of property

speculation that gave great wealth to those who were successful. Okehampton, Lydford and Tavistock and many other communities were given charters to develop as towns. The speculations were particularly successful where tin and cloth trades developed to provide a year-round base and a focus for the markets and fairs that moved around the country. At this time, both Plymouth and Dartmouth were founded as ship-building centres because ships were needed not only for defence but also for the vital role of trade.

The early Middle Ages saw much activity in Devon. The tin ore, untouched since its formation 300 million years before, was plundered. As a tin rush developed and a Klondyke fever set in, local landowners set up towns (the famous Stannary Towns) at strategic points to weigh and stamp the tin. Many of these remain important towns to this day. Mining was to have a devastating effect on some parts of the country as miners turned over the river gravels (a process called streaming), looking for tin ore. They worked their way up

Lydford Castle, one of the earliest strongholds built to guard this difficult country, was mainly used as a prison (Walk 7)

stream until they found the ore-rich seam (lode) and then dug pits and shafts and left waste heaps as they followed the lode across the open moor (e.g. Warren House and Vitrifer Mine, Walk 10).

Alongside all this farming and commercial activity rose the great religious houses that became established at such places as Buckfast, Buckland, Torre and Tavistock. It was they who established sheep runs on the moor, ensuring that the forest would never again re-establish. They also founded many of Devon's finest churches.

The last changes wrought by the hand of man began in the 18th century. First there was a revival of mining, which had died down by the end of the Middle Ages. This time, the mining was for copper, tungsten, iron and silver rather than for tin. The mines opened on the west of Dartmoor near Tavistock proved to be the richest in the country. By the beginning of the 19th century, the trade had grown so fast that a canal was specially built to link Tavistock with the Tamar at Morwellham (now a special conservation area, Morwellham Quay). By the 1850s these mines were producing half the world's copper.

At this time the Tamar valley was buzzing with activity, 300-ton ships could reach Morwellham, and crushing mills, furnaces and much other processing plant lined the banks and the mine sites. However, it was a period that could not last: copper from the best lodes was worked out and falling prices made further exploration uneconomic. Today, the only signs of this once world-famous industry are the derelict chimney stacks of the mine engine houses and the partly overgrown spoil heaps (View 3).

As the tide of the Industrial Revolution washed over Devon it barely changed the countryside because there was little coal to power machines. The coal to drive the engines of the copper mines had to be imported from Wales. Devon was largely a supplier of raw material to the industries located elsewhere in Britain, providing, in addition to copper, large amounts of china clay from great open quarries at Shaugh Prior near Plymouth. It was the railway that most altered the face of Devon, for it opened up new markets for the farmers and fishermen of the county, establishing the dairy farming and market gardening that are now so much part of the Devon scene and ensuring the growth of harbours like Brixham which, by the beginning of the 20th century, had no less than 300 trawlers for catching herring and pilchard. However, although 'export' markets were important, the railway also opened up the country to people from outside, and the age of tourism began.

Devon had always been a difficult county to cross. Its deep, steep-sided valleys and long estuaries made communications slow and arduous and required extensive bridge building. At first, bridges were simple slabs of stone (the moorland 'clapper bridges', see Walk 5) but later true, arched, stone bridges were constructed. The same difficulties initially deterred even railway engineers, yet by 1848 the

(Opposite) **Abbeys played an important role in the structure of moorland and village; their flocks prevented trees from recolonising the moor and their priests founded many of the village churches: Buckfast Abbey is a new building but an ancient foundation (Drive 2)**

railway had stretched as far as Torquay and Plymouth. It was the railway that led directly to the growth of new towns. People moved to them from the countryside, which caused the demise of much arable farming, and the rise of pastoral agriculture. Only towns on the railway route survived; the others gradually declined. Today there is still a great contrast between these quiet, peaceful and not very prosperous rural centres and the bustling seaside resorts.

Visits to the seaside were begun by a certain Dr Russell who published a book called 'On glandular consumption and the use of sea water in diseases of the glands'. He established a fashion for visiting the seaside which, although it started with the rich in the days before the railway, became available to all. South Devon became particularly important for holiday-makers because its splendid sandy beaches are mostly sheltered from prevailing westerly winds. However, each seaside town has developed in a different way. Torquay, for example, was planned for the middle and upper classes of Victorian England and, for a long time, tried to protect itself from the working classes and day trippers. Here the broad avenues are lined with palm trees, roads are contoured up the hills to provide large residential houses with the best views, and there are planned formal gardens. In contrast, nearby Paignton, once a small village over half a mile from the sea, grew specifically to cater for the working classes and the day trippers. Thus it acquired rows of guest-houses laid out in the more traditional grid-iron pattern so common in Victorian towns.

(Opposite) **Trade brought prosperity to many moor-edge villages and inns were needed to provide shelter for travellers (Drive 2)**

South Devon weather

Planning holidays well in advance involves taking pot luck with the weather. Day by day, however, it is possible to choose a walk or drive that will be pleasant and attractive even under cloudy and rainy skies. This chapter will help you to understand a little of what causes South Devon weather, to forecast what might be in store for the day ahead, and to make the most of your stay.

We will start with some obvious differences within South Devon that exist irrespective of the general weather. The temperature falls as you go higher, so on the coast at Torquay it might be 68°F (20°C) whereas on High Willhays Tor the same sun will only raise the air temperature to perhaps 62°F (17°C). As a rule of thumb you can always expect temperatures to fall by about 3°F (about 1.8°C) for every 1000 ft (300 m) of ascent. There is another obvious change in the weather between sheltered and exposed places. In a valley, air may be motionless but you can almost guarantee there will be a breeze on the cliff-tops and in many cases a fair wind on the tors. A drop in temperature or a strong breeze may bring you out in goose pimples, so the combination of cool air and breeze creates effects far more severe than the simple sum of the two. Scientists call the loss of body heat under these circumstances windchill, which in its most severe form is commonly known as exposure. However, in Devon, the only places where you need to take special care (except in winter) would be on the moors. In these cases it is common sense to guard against the changes that occur between sheltered valley and exposed moor by taking a sweater with you.

In weather terms, South Devon is a particularly favoured part of Britain, as indeed Britain is a particularly favoured area of the world. For example, whereas deep snows pile up during winter in Ottawa, Canada, the town of Torquay, at the same latitude, is 20°F (11°C) warmer and rarely sees even a flurry of snow. The difference is entirely a result of the warm waters that drift across the Atlantic from the Gulf of Mexico to bathe Britain's West Coast. As winds blow over the warm water they too become warmer and give the temperate winters that make out-of-season holidays or retirement in South Devon so attractive. The mild winters and early springs also allow palm trees to flourish on the promenade at Torquay, and enable local growers to produce some of the earliest vegetables in the country.

The mild air is a constant advantage to South Devon and even Dartmoor, but the same wind that influences the temperature is also responsible for day-to-day changes in the weather. Because most of Britain's weather is brought by winds blowing from the Atlantic, it pays to look westwards for any signs of a change. As the air skims over the thousands of miles of ocean between Britain and America, it becomes increasingly moist. The amount of moisture it can hold depends on how warm the air is; because air reaching Britain's West

(Opposite) **Early trade was mainly concerned with wool and in many places water-powered mills were built, similar to this one at Dartington (Drive 2)**

Coast is forced to rise, it cools, thereby reducing its capacity for moisture.

The chances of rain depend on altitude and exposure to the westerly winds. Thus Plymouth has about 40 in (around 1000 mm) of rain a year and the high moorland village of Princetown 82 in (2082 mm), but Exeter, sheltered partly from the rain by the mass of Dartmoor, has only 30 in (750 mm). Nevertheless, the amount of moisture that the air must shed on any one occasion is very hard to predict. If you are lucky, it will be no more than is needed to produce small clouds; if you are less lucky, a bit more will condense and the clouds will begin to merge; and if you are really unlucky, the clouds will be unable to hold all the excess moisture and then you will need an umbrella (or, on the moors, more sensibly a waterproof nylon coat).

It is the unpredictability of the cloud that makes the weather fore-caster's job so difficult. In any case, the forecast you hear on the radio applies mainly to lowland areas: it may not be very appropriate for the moors. Better, therefore, to phone for the local weather (dial Plymouth (0752) 8091) or read the sky for yourself as outlined in the diagrams that follow.

Making the most of the weather

Beaches may be wonderful during sunny weather but can be miserable in cloud or rain. Cloudy days are, however, quite suitable for walking on cliff-tops or moors, when a cool breeze may even be a comfort. Remember also that waterfalls are actually at their best just after rain.

There are ways of making a reasonable guess at the prospects to enable you to plan your day. You can begin by trying to decide if the weather is likely to get better or worse through the day. If you stand with your back to the wind, worsening weather will be on your left, so a southerly wind and a partly cloudy sky may foretell more cloud or rain, whereas a wind from the north suggests that clearing skies will soon appear and you can expect no more than the occasional shower. If there is no distinct wind, the chances are that the weather will remain constant.

Most winds over Devon blow from the south-west and the worst of Britain's weather passes by to the north. A southwesterly wind also means that most coastal beaches, such as Torbay and Babbacombe, will be quite sheltered, and only those west of Start Point can expect an onshore breeze. Fortunately, all beaches are sheltered from the cool north winds, which are the nightmare of North Devon coastal resorts. It is this, perhaps above all else, that makes the resorts of the South Devon coast among the most popular in Britain.

Dartmoor causes air to rise and cloud to form with some regularity. Depending on the height at which moisture condenses on any particular day, this can be seen as low cloud, mist or fog. On the

(Opposite) **Long estuaries still cause much isolation in South Devon, and even important towns like Dartmouth still rely heavily on ferries (Drive 1)**

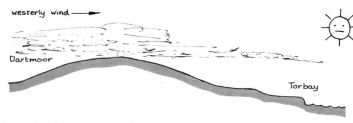

(a) Uniform layers of grey cloud over moor and coast are unlikely to clear quickly: avoid routes on the high moors and try the coast (Walks 2, 3, 13, Drive 1) where you may at least find hazy sunshine

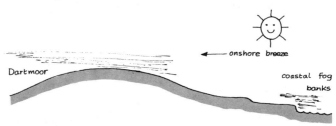

(b) Coastal fog usually only extends inland for a few miles, although the moist air it portends may also give cloud on the moors: try spending the morning between the two, say at Lydford (Walk 7)

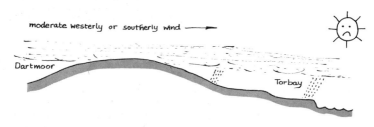

(c) Sheets of light, uniform cloud, covering the sky evenly belong to a depression which may not bring rain over lowland, but over the moors rain is more certain and the cloud is unlikely to disperse: try using the morning for shopping and have a leisurely pub lunch followed by a drive (Drive 2)

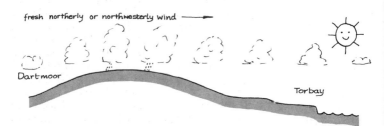

(d) Billowing clouds that start to build from a sparkling clear sky in the early morning may cause overcast sky by midday (this will happen first on the moors) and rain showers are likely in the afternoon, but between the showers the rain-washed air gives crystal-clear visibility and interesting cloud shadows: this is good weather for photographing landscapes, especially the moors in the morning (Walks 4, 5, 9, 10)

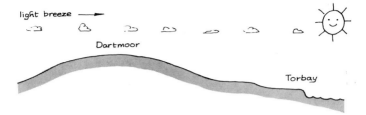

light breeze ⟶

Dartmoor

Torbay

(e) Small white 'cotton wool' clouds, which float in the sky but do not grow, are a guarantee of fine sunny weather everywhere: visibility will be good, and these 'fun clouds' highlight the sky for landscape photography

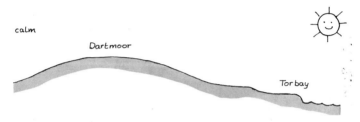

calm

Dartmoor

Torbay

(f) A hot sunny period of settled weather over coast and moor is foretold by the rhyme 'red sky at night, shepherd's delight', for a red sky is caused by the rays of the setting sun being bounced off tiny dust particles in the air, and dust only accumulates like this under a region of high pressure: good weather for all routes and with the certainty of a good sizzle on the beach.

Have a nice day!

moors, mist and fog (cloud at ground level) are not easily dispersed and you would do better to seek the lower ground by the coast.

Fog is also common along most of Britain's coasts. In summer it is most often produced when warm, moist air from tropical regions is blown over the relatively cool water of the English Channel. South Devon coastal fog is therefore almost always associated with an onshore wind. These 'sea breezes' have an unpleasant habit of rolling in fog-banks to shroud the coast, especially in early morning. However, they are usually of very limited extent; inland the sky will most probably be clear and the sun will be shining. So, if you wake up to the sound of a foghorn on the coast, head for the hills. Drive just a few miles inland and you may be able to look down on the fog-enveloped coast while you bathe in warm sunshine. Coastal fog is often dispersed by the warming effects of the sun and has usually thinned considerably by lunchtime. The afternoon is likely to be sunny and warm although, if the fog has lasted to lunchtime, this means the sun has not been able to warm coastal air very quickly and the afternoon will remain cool.

PART 2   ROUTES

Views: getting your bearings

1 From Haytor Rocks

Introduction

Standing guard like a lone sentinel on the eastern approaches of Dartmoor Forest, the distinctive granite eminence of Hay Tor (1490 ft; 454 m) is one of the most visited of all Devon tors, partly, perhaps, because it is near a road, but also because

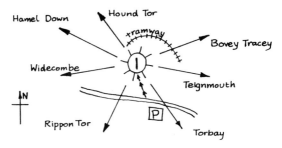

The view from Hay Tor

it is not (as are so many tors) just a jumble of boulders but a tightly interlocked and upright mass, a natural fortress which is a delight to see and a magnificent spot from which to get your bearings.

The view

Although Hay Tor lies at the eastern end of the great granite dome that forms the core of Dartmoor, there is still a real feeling of being within the moor. From the foot of the tor stones – and even better from their top – you can see the grass- and heather-covered moorland stretch far away, each gentle rise crowned with its own tor stones. Most prominently to the south lies the slightly higher Rippon Tor (1560 ft; 475 m), and immediately north is Hound Tor (Walk 9), which, although it barely reaches 1400 ft (427 m), is none the less imposing. However, it is to the west where the highest land lies, and here the horizon is dominated by the broad ridge of Hamel Down (about 1700 ft; 518 m), which overlooks the famous moorland village of Widecombe.

It may seem that tors must be an ancient part of the landscape, but only a few tens of thousands of years ago – before the Ice Age – Dartmoor was a

➔ Hay Tor is near Bovey Tracey off the A38(T) Exeter to Plymouth road. At Bovey B3344 [Manaton >]. On hill fork left [Hay Tor >]. Hay Tor **P** **WC** Footpath to tor

From Haytor Rocks 31

land without tors and the granite we see today was buried under many tens of feet of soil. Now it can be warm and sunny on many a summer day, but during the Ice Age the moorland was only just beyond the reach of huge glaciers that had come down from northern Britain and were pushing against the North Devon cliffs. At this time, Hay Tor was a cold, barren place, even in the height of summer, but the whole landscape was not completely locked in an icy prison because each summer a temporary thaw set in. Try to imagine the scene. All around, snow is steadily melting, revealing occasional patches of bare, dark, water-soaked soil. Only a few inches beneath the surface, the soil remains frozen, so each drip from the melting snow helps to turn the topsoil into mud. Gradually, under its own weight, this mud begins to tear away from the still-frozen soil below, sliding and flowing into the valley bottoms. Year after year the process is repeated until the hilltop soil is stripped away, the valleys are partly filled, and the solid granite boulders become exposed. Now it is the turn of the granite to feel the full force of the weather; ice forms in cracks between the blocks, wedging them apart; some blocks shatter and fall away to litter the hill slope with angular rubble (called clitter), leaving only the largest and toughest granite blocks to survive. Today, Hay Tor still stands because it is formed from the largest and toughest blocks in east Dartmoor, whereas most nearby tors have been reduced virtually to rubble. Since this time soil has formed once more on the valley slopes and the clitter is slowly being covered by grass, heather and bracken; now only the tors remain as they were when the ice sheets melted 12000 years ago.

The toughness of the granite has ensured that, whatever the agents of erosion, it remained higher than the encircling landscape. From Hay Tor you can clearly see the rounded hills of this lower land stretching beyond Bovey Tracey, a landscape deeply trenched by rivers collecting their waters from the moorland. Hills of uniform height and deep valleys give this countryside the appearance of a series of parallel ridges. Whereas tough granite yields thin, poor soils and is under heather, the more easily weathered lowland has the deep, fertile, red soils that are so much a part of the Devon scene, divided by high earth banks into a chequerboard of small fields. Whereas tree planting has been strenuously opposed on the moor, on the steep sides of the valleys beyond there are extensive forests, some of them serried rows of conifer plantations. Fortunately, however, many others are broadleaved trees (see Walk 6).

From earliest times, people have recognised the landmark of Hay Tor. Bronze Age people built their turf and wood shelters on its flanks and their characteristic oval burial mounds (tumuli) are still a prominent moorland feature. Despite the worsening climate, people continued to live on the moors until medieval times; on the flanks of nearby Hound Tor (Walk 9) a village survived well into the Middle Ages, despite the fact that winters were even more severe than at present.

The last people to use the moor before the days of the holiday-maker were the quarrymen. The grass-covered winding ridge in the valley beyond the quarry marks the line of the 'railway' built specially to carry the granite away. It is made from blocks of granite scored with deep grooves in which the wooden truck wheels ran. Horses pulled the trucks and their heavy loads filled barges on the Stover Canal in the nearby Bovey Valley. From the quarry the piers for London's Tower Bridge were hewn, and giant blocks were carried away to build the Eddystone Lighthouse. Visit the quarry (there is a guard fence, but take care – the sides are sheer), where you can see the rock that lies at Dartmoor's heart. The massive blocks of granite have withstood the ravages not only of Ice Age weather but also of the erosion that took place over aeons of time before that. These blocks have long been used by man for building, but he had to toil hard to hew them.

2   From Torbay to Hope's Nose

Introduction

The coast of South Devon is one of the most richly varied in Britain. Here, rocks of many differing colours, compositions and origins have been stood on end and are so arranged that each juts out to sea. Some are weak and have succumbed to the power of storm waves driven in from the Atlantic; others, made from sterner stuff, have survived the onslaught and today stand proud as headlands. One of these headlands, Hope's Nose, lies just to the north of Torquay and provides a splendid place,

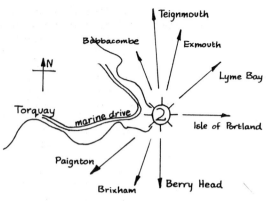

The view from Hope's Nose

From Torquay centre, follow coast road north (Marine Drive) first [Meadfoot >]. Hope's Nose is the end of the headland beyond Meadfoot. From clifftop [public footpath >] to headland. From 🅿 opposite island of Thatcher Rock (Frontispiece) follow coast footpath to Hope's Nose; 1 mile (0.6 km), ½ hour

both from cliff-top and from the shore, to look along a great expanse of one of Britain's most beautiful coasts.

The view

Hope's Nose is the most easterly part of an intricate pattern of coves and headlands that form the northern jaws of Torbay. However, to see Torbay and appreciate the landscape, it is best to walk at a leisurely pace from opposite Thatcher Rock to the coastguard station on the Nose itself.

Thatcher Rock, a small islet just a few hundred yards from the coast, looks as though it is crowned by a natural castle. It is this 'castle' that offers an important clue to the nature of the South Devon coast. See how the prominent rock band that makes the 'ramparts' tilts steeply towards the sea: all the nearby rocks are similarly arranged. Now trace a line to continue these ramparts towards the right. This line does not, as you might at first suppose, come directly on shore but, instead, heads westwards across Meadfoot Bay, only gaining the mainland at the southern headland. Indeed, all the rocks of Torbay are aligned in an east–west fashion, which means that, as we continue to walk eastwards along the headland towards Hope's Nose, none of the small islets is of the same rock as those underfoot. Instead they trace out lines of tough rock that run parallel to the present coast. Today, they remain as isolated fragments of a band of rock mostly washed away by the sea, but their continued presence is a dramatic witness to the power of the waves and shows just how much land has been lost in the past.

Views 34

The rocks of Meadfoot Bay and, to a lesser extent, the coves along the headland, are formed in bands that are weaker for one reason or another than those making the headlands. Meadfoot Bay, for example, is backed by easily eroded grey shales (rocks made from mud), whereas much of the headland is made from tougher slates. In the past, all the rocks have been squashed and contorted, as is vividly shown in the cliffs opposite Thatcher Rock. Here you can see, cut across by the waves, a slice of the cliffs that were once under so much pressure that they folded over on themselves. These curved bands of rock were once flat sheets! The nearby bay displays a wide variety of rock bands; some are red, some blue, and others brownish grey. These rocks, too, have been fractured and broken up, although some have fared better than others. Little wonder, therefore, that some have been easily eroded and formed into coves by gale-lashed winter waves.

Across the far side of Torbay lies Berry Head (Walk 13). This, too, is formed in steeply tilted rocks although, from a distance, the flat cliff-top suggests quite the opposite. Flat-topped cliffs are a common feature of the South Devon coast; they have all been cut across by the sea at a time when the land was lower. Once the top of Berry Head was a beach and the hills to its right were a cliff, as indeed was the headland on which you stand.

Notice how many large ships lie at anchor in Tor Bay – a marine equivalent of a lorry park – chosen simply because the bay is deep and provides such good natural shelter from the fiercest of the Atlantic gales. Whole navies have sheltered in this bay, including large contingents waiting to make the Normandy landings during the Second World War.

Hope's Nose, easily distinguished because of its attraction for fishermen, shows the scars of extensive quarrying. It has paid the price for being a resistant limestone rock band, because it has caught the eye of people anxious to find tough stone for road foundations and buildings.

The Nose provides a vantage point for sweeping views northwards to Teignmouth on the estuary of the River Teign; to Dawlish near the estuary of the River Exe, and even as far as Dorset. The huge red sandstone cliffs in the distance are the last in Devon, the sandstone a reminder of the time when this area was a desert. In great contrast are the rocks of Black Head near at hand, whose black knobbly form tells of another time when volcanoes poured fiery rivers of lava across the landscape. Here, as everywhere in South Devon, variety is the keynote.

3   From Kit Hill near Plymouth

Introduction
Kit Hill lies just across the Tamar river in Cornwall. It is an isolated conical hill with a granite core, which reminds us that granite not only lies beneath Dartmoor, but also appears intermittently at the surface westwards through Cornwall to the Scilly

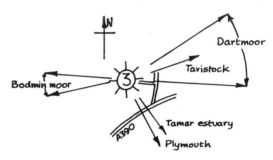

The view from Kit Hill

Isles. However, Kit Hill is the only exposure of granite between Dartmoor and Bodmin Moor and is the only high ground for 10 miles (16 km) in any direction. On a fine day it is an excellent place to get your bearings.

The view
The great mass of molten rock that slowly rose from deep within the Earth and finally solidified to make the granite of Devon and Cornwall has a very lumpy upper surface. Each lump forms one of the moors (in comparison to which Kit Hill is a mere pimple), and between them the granite still lies buried beneath many hundreds of feet of other rock. When the granite was still molten, boiling liquids, some at temperatures over 1000°C, flowed up through the overlying sheets of rock, pushing their way through cracks in sandstone, shale and limestone and slowly cooling from liquids into solids. Thus were formed, in the rocks overlying the granite, the rich lodes of tin, zinc, copper and other metal ores for which the area has become so famous.

While the fluids were pushing their way through the overlying rocks, the heat given off by the granite was so intense that it literally baked all the

➤ From Plymouth [Tamar Bridge >] then A388 [Callington >]. At Callington right A390 [Tavistock >]. In 3 miles (5 km) [Kit Hill >] on left. From Tavistock A390 [Callington >]. In 8 miles (13 km) [Kit Hill >] on right. Easily distinguished by large chimney on hilltop

Views   36

rocks surrounding it. Shales were melted and their crystals rearranged into shining plates of mica, which is a common constituent of a glistening rock called schist. Sandstones were melted down to white bands of quartzite and limestones were baked into marble. Although the rocks were thus hardened, over aeons of time they have been slowly worn away until now the tops of the granite have begun to show through. Some of these overlying rocks contained the rich metal ore which, because it is heavy, remained in river beds until it was found by the miners 'streaming' the rivers; most, however, was washed completely away.

At Kit Hill the overlying rocks have still not been stripped from the granite and many of them have not yielded their riches. It was for this reason that most miners came to the area near Kit Hill rather than on to Dartmoor itself.

When you look out from Kit Hill, to the east you see the great mass of Dartmoor, its unmistakable brown-grey shadow dominating the horizon. To the west is the more subdued granite mass of Bodmin Moor, which helps to form the spine of Cornwall. By contrast, to north and south, where the molten granite did not rise as high, the landscape is much lower and it retains many of the overlying rocks. As a result it is more fertile than the nearby moors and, instead of brownish heather growing on poor, acid soils, there is a patchwork of green pastures growing on fertile clay lands. Into these covering rocks the River Tamar and its tributaries have trenched deeply, cutting the imposing gorge at Gunnislake whose precipitous cliffs were an obstacle to the miners who needed to ship out their ore from the river below. Near Plymouth the deeply trenched valley has now been drowned and formed into an estuary whose waters can be seen glistening in the sun, a shimmering signpost to the docks of Devonport.

Kit Hill presents the two aspects so typical of the landscapes of South Devon: on the one hand there is the variety of nature as she works to etch out the many rocks, each with its different toughness; and on the other hand there is man, so evident on the moor-edge scene eking a living from the soil and, in the past, from deep in the rocks beneath.

The stack of the old Kit Hill Mine, which crowns the summit of Kit Hill, is a memorial to the centuries of speculation and effort that went into mining, first for tin and later copper, arsenic, zinc, fluorspar and wolfram. Kit Hill was near the centre of the mining area and in every direction the derelict and ruined chimneys of pumping engines and winding gear abound. Near this spot, fortunes were made by those lucky enough to discover rich veins of ore, and fortunes lost by those still working the lodes when they ran out or when world prices fell. In the nearby Tamar valley, industry once lined the now peaceful banks and a substantial port – Morwellham (now a museum) – grew and was sustained.

Lodes nearly always ran in an east–west direction, influenced by the pattern of fractures produced by ancient mountain building. Rarely was it possible to follow a lode horizontally into the hillside (although there are two tunnels (adits) over 1000 ft (300 m) long under Kit Hill). Instead most mines had to follow the ore downwards in lodes that might be no more than a few inches thick. The area is dotted with deep, narrow clefts; around Kit Hill they are fenced off, but you must still take care, for many are several hundred feet deep.

Although mining continued until early this century, there are now few signs of the labours of thousands of miners in times past. Only the hand of the quarryman remains visible where, on the north side of Kit Hill, the quarry walls show the massive blocks of granite that form the core of the hill. Look at the wide variety of crystals in the rock – pink, yellow and white opaque feldspar crystals, often several inches long; small shining plates of black mica; and the glassy sheen of quartz. It is these minerals, never of commercial value, that, now the ore has gone, provide a wealth of interest to many who visit Kit Hill or the nearby moors.

(Opposite) **Dartmoor roads**

DARTMOOR
Which roads to use

uitable for·

HOST
ehicles

MEDIUM
ehicles
(no caravans)

CARS & SMALL
ehicles only

LOCAL access

Black routes ❯

Blue routes ❯

Brown routes ❯

Other routes ❯

Drives in and around South Devon

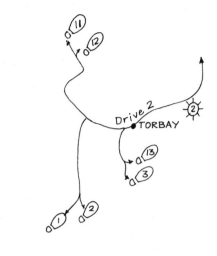

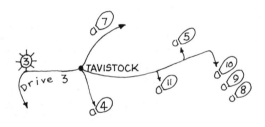

Routes from Torbay and Tavistock

1 The southern moor and coast

Introduction

The area lying to the south of Dartmoor is called the South Hams peninsula. Despite the moderate, even height of the plateau of South Hams (between 500 and 600 ft; 150 and 180 m), the land is everywhere deeply trenched by swift-flowing streams, which drain from the rain-soaked slopes of Dartmoor. Indeed, so steep are many valley sides that they remain forested to this day, undeveloped in one of the most climatically favoured parts of Britain. Travellers have found the valleys equally arduous, preferring the relatively easy land at the foot of the moor. But the real isolation of the area is created by the estuaries of the Rivers Erme, Avon and Dart, which send watery fingers up to 10 miles (16 km) inland, requiring the traveller to make tortuous detours to reach the coast.

The features of the countryside that have tended to isolate South Hams have allowed it to retain a natural charm that is so hard to find in modern Britain. Towns and villages remain small and uncluttered by extensive suburbs, and roads are largely free of heavy traffic. Here you will find twisting country roads that present a constantly changing scene: sometimes of distant moor, sometimes of rolling plateau and steep, wooded valley, and every so often a glimpse of glistening waters of an estuary or the sea.

The final part of the drive visits the southwestern shoulders of Dartmoor, an area quite different in many respects from most of the moor. Here, hundreds of millions of years ago, the newly formed granite began to be weathered by the same fluids that elsewhere were penetrating into the overlying rocks and depositing valuable minerals. These minerals were formed near Plymouth but mostly the rocks have long been eroded away, exposing the product of weathered granite called china clay. From the level of the moonscape quarries you can see out over South Hams and Plymouth to the Eddystone Rocks, some 17 miles (27 km) off the coast, their famous lighthouse perched on a small outlying reef of Devon's oldest rocks, sturdily built of Hay Tor granite.

The drive

➥ From Plymouth A38 [Exeter >]. At Ivybridge take B3211 [Ermington >]

The main Plymouth to Exeter road (A38) skirts the edge of Dartmoor, giving a contrast between the tor-capped and heather-covered moors on the left and the pastureland of the plateau of South Hams to the right.

At Ivybridge, the waters of the River Erme funnel down from their source on Dartmoor and cut a valley southwards across the South Hams plateau, which, in this area, lies at about 500 ft (150 m).

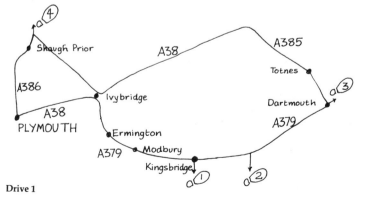

Drive 1

Although the underlying rocks are rarely seen peeking from beneath the chequerboard of pasture and arable fields, their influence on man and the countryside is remarkable. Rocks occur in alternating weak and strong bands across the course of the Erme, a pattern reflected in the dog-leg path followed by the river. Wherever there is a weak rock, the valley is wide; wherever it cuts south through harder rock, only a narrow steep-sided valley forms.

The River Erme's tributaries have etched the soft and hard rocks in a similar manner, flowing either from south-west to north-east or south, dividing the whole plateau into diamond-shaped hills. Such a landscape offers two choices: follow the valleys with dog-legged routes or ride across the ridges as far as possible, diving down into the valleys and back up again as required. Neither course is entirely satisfactory, but the many twists and turns, and rises and falls along your route clearly show that a variety of solutions have been adopted.

Ermington
🅿 wc ♿ 🅿 ⊘

The harder rock bands of South Hams are grey and brown speckled shales. You may not see them in the countryside, but they are everywhere in the older houses, as walls and roofs.

In Ermington turn right, then A379 [Modbury, Kingsbridge >]

Very few villages occupy valley-bottom sites, where the land is wet and often marshy. For example, the houses in Ermington and Modbury keep well clear not only of wet land but also of areas liable to winter floods. Only the mill, which formerly used water power, occupies a waterside site, and even here a fast-flowing hillside stream was preferred to a valley-bottom location using the larger, but slower, main river.

Modbury
🅿 wc ♿ 🏨 🍴 🅿 ⊘

From Modbury the road travels alongside a tributary stream until it gains the plateau top. From this vantage point, the remarkably even skyline of the plateau shows clearly. Having thus risen over a ridge, the road falls slowly, using another tributary to reach the valley of the River Avon. This route from Ermington is of particular interest because it keeps well inland, connecting the lowest bridging points of the rivers whose estuaries bite deep into the coastline: there are no through-roads seawards of the Ermington to Kingsbridge road. Indeed, Kingsbridge, which lies more than 5 miles (8 km)

(Opposite) **The main street of Modbury, built largely away from the wet valley bottom on a road that joins two ridge routes**

Kingsbridge
🅿 wc ♨ 🏨 🍴 🅿 ⊘
For ⚓, 🅿 by
quayside gardens.
(A381 [Salcombe >]
for Walk 1)

inland at the head of the particularly wide and tortuous Kingsbridge estuary, derives its name from its river crossing position where a bridge was built to connect two royal estates.

At Kingsbridge there is a particularly good opportunity to appreciate the relationship between town, land and sea. From the quayside gardens you can look back and see the houses of the town clustered on the sides of the little valleys and coming to an abrupt stop by the tidal limit. However, the sharp end to the estuary is artificial and is produced by reclaiming the valley floor that now lies beyond the bus station. By so doing, people not only obtained more land for building but also could bring their quay right into town.

At both Aveton Gifford and Kingsbridge the valley sides dip down into the tidal muds and salt marshes at quite abrupt angles. Geographers call these estuaries rias, believing them to be relics of a time, during the Ice Age, when rivers cut down deeply to lower levels only to be drowned when the ice melted and the sea level rose. Now sea water laps the valley sides and rivers have begun to infill their valleys again. At Kingsbridge you can see how nearly they have succeeded in the 12 000 years since the ice melted: at low tide the estuary becomes one vast mud flat. Of course, extensive silting discourages shipping, which is the reason Kingsbridge could never develop to become an important harbour, but it is a good place to look at a wide variety of wading birds.

The death knell for Kingsbridge was tolled by the railway, which stretched down from Plymouth in 1893 and took the active coastal trade away. Today, Kingsbridge relies on holiday-makers to boost its trade; as well as its central position for visitors to South Hams it has an attractive shopping arcade, The Shambles, whose Elizabethan-age bays are supported on granite piers.

A379 [Torcross,
Dartmouth >]

The coast is first reached at Tor Cross, the southern end of a large shingle ridge called Slapton Sands. Here 2 miles (3 km) of cliff are divorced from the sea behind a lagoon of brackish water called

(At Stokenham turn
right for Walk 2
[Start Point >])

Slapton Ley. (Slapton is Saxon for 'marshy place'.) This is a unique part of Britain's countryside, not least because it contains an important nature reserve.

The main road runs across the shingle bar, a far

(Opposite) **The graceful curve of Slapton Sands, which traps the lagoon of Slapton Ley: Start Point lies in the distance**

easier route than along the deeply trenched cliff-top. However, the bar is not very wide, which makes its survival seem all the more remarkable. The shingle is able to remain in place because its rough surface can withstand the force of the storm waves. Nevertheless, Slapton Sands is not growing at present; it is a relic feature built by the rising sea at the end of the Ice Age. At nearby Hallsands (Walk 2) there is striking evidence of the disastrous impact of man on such fragile beaches. The American armed forces used Slapton Sands for beach landing practice between 1943 and 1944; there is a commemorative obelisk by the road midway along the bar.

From Slapton the road rises to the cliff-top, giving a bird's-eye view over the curving lines of the shingle bar and its lagoon. This is a slow ponderous road, which clearly illustrates the difficulties of adopting a cliff-top route in South Devon, its sole purpose being to reach the River Dart estuary and the ferry at Dartmouth.

Dartmouth 🅿 **WC** ♿
🐕 🚻 PO Ø **M**
Ferry to Torbay and
Walk 3

Dartmouth town lies beside an estuary which, unlike Kingsbridge, has not been filled with sediment. Indeed, Dartmouth is famous for its deep water and sheltered harbour. For long it has been an important naval base, with the Royal Naval College very prominent on the right of the road to Totnes. However, Dartmouth did not grow beside the water; rather it was established on top of the hill, 400 ft (122 m) above the water at Townstall. It was not until the 13th century that two small fishing hamlets below Townstall combined into the embryo port on the only flat land around.

Everything about Dartmouth reflects its famous maritime history: Smith Street, the street of the smiths where metal ship parts were made and repaired, was once on the water's edge, so you can see that much of Dartmouth is built on reclaimed land. Just down stream lie the twin forts that protected the harbour; one on each side of the estuary because the guns could not fire completely across. When better guns were developed in the 17th century, the Kingswear fort was abandoned.

The reason that there is so much to see in Dartmouth is that the tide of industrialisation has never washed over the town. Strong local objection prevented the railway engineers from bridging the River Dart inland and the best they could do was to

(Opposite) **The character of Dartmouth has largely been preserved by its isolation**

bring a branch from Torbay to Kingswear on the opposite bank. The estuary is too wide for a bridge, which means that ferries still have to be used, and there is little flat land for industry. There are not even any sandy beaches nearby to allow its development as a major tourist resort. Perhaps for all of these reasons Dartmouth retains its quiet charm.

A381 [Totnes >]

By contrast, bustling Totnes lies at the head of the Dart estuary, separated from Dartmouth by the now familiar deeply trenched plateau. Totnes could be reached by railway and its central position in South Devon meant that its future was assured. The buildings of the medieval town, still retained within its red sandstone walls, are aligned on the hillside from the castle stronghold downwards. Below lies Totnes Quay, the port on the River Dart that was used in the export of wool and cloth in the Middle Ages. The Guildhall – the centre of the wool trade – a piazza (covered walk) and many other fine buildings still survive. Today, bacon and cider have taken over from wool, but although the town centre bustles with shoppers, the medieval character of the town and even the old town gates still remain.

Totnes 🅿 (castle) **WC**
🍴🍺🚌 [PO] 🚫 ⛰ 🚾
(Dart Valley Steam
Railway) **M** ℹ

A385 [Plymouth >]
then A38 to
Ivybridge.
At Ivybridge
[Cornwood,
Yelverton >]

All through the journey across South Hams, Dartmoor has not been far away, and from most hill crests its broad back can be seen outlined against the sky. South Hams is a much more prosperous area than the moor, as is readily apparent on the final part of the route.

Ivybridge is only a small market town lying at the junction of upland and lowland. To the north stretches the bleak upland region to which no major roads venture. Indeed much of the trade for Ivybridge was brought by the Plymouth to Exeter road (A38), which crossed the River Erme here.

Shaugh Moor 🌿

The Dartmoor countryside beyond Ivybridge is quite different from South Hams. The deep, red soils disappear and are replaced by shallow, brown soils of low fertility; the rich pasturelands give way to rough grazing and eventually to heather moor, which is of such low quality that it requires regular burning simply to allow grass to grow at all. The size of Cornwood reflects the lack of prosperity along the moor edge. It is simply a cluster of houses at a crossing of two minor roads: it was never a suitable site for industry. Yet industry has come to the moor edge because, just north of Cornwood and near to the moorside hamlet of Shaugh Prior, lies a major deposit of china clay.

[Shaugh Prior,
Bickleigh >], then
A386 [Plymouth >]

You cannot miss the devastated landscape of

Shaugh Moor. The huge piles of white spoil, the lakes filling the bottoms of deep pits, the roadways and tramways all crowd against the road to show the effects of large-scale extractive industry. Indeed, the extent of the operations is so great that these man-made forms take on an interest and character of their own. Nevertheless, Shaugh Moor has retained some of its rural character and the moor shoulder provides a splendid bird's-eye view southwards across Plymouth, Devonport and the Tamar estuary.

Shaugh Prior (Saxon for 'a place in a copse'; Walk 4) is another hamlet whose growth has been limited by the poor agricultural prospects around. It is a true moor-edge settlement, for beyond it lie the softer rocks that surround the granite and into which the River Plym has cut the spectacular gorge that separates Bickleigh from the moor. It is the isolation of Shaugh Prior on one side of the wooded valley that has kept it free from suburban expansion; it is the accessibility of Bickleigh on the edge of Plymouth that could cause it to be overwhelmed.

2 The eastern moor and coast

Introduction

The eastern side of Dartmoor is much more intensively settled than the west. The Romans built a major fort just east of Dartmoor at Exeter, from where they tentatively explored westwards. In the Middle Ages, Exeter grew into a flourishing port and market centre, drawing to itself the products of a rich agricultural land that stretched to the slopes of Dartmoor. The lowlands east of the moor are favoured areas for agriculture because they are protected from the worst of the westerly gales and rainfall by the great mass of moorland, leaving them with summers far warmer and drier than those on the windward west. When the railway advanced westwards, the easier route through South Devon was chosen, allowing farm goods to reach distant markets and urban dwellers the warm, sunny, Devon coasts. For both historic and contemporary reasons, therefore, the eastern moors and coast have become a more bustling region than any other part of the moorland fringe. But this has not meant dull uniformity. Rather it has enhanced the variety of places of interest: there are wide, sheltered, sandy beaches and seaside resorts such as Torbay, busy market towns like Totnes, or working centres such as Newton Abbot.

Ease of access to the moorland fringe has, however, had little impact on Dartmoor. As soon as the moorland is reached beyond Bovey Tracey, the soft, warm, intensively settled landscape is replaced by a wild, open, sparsely peopled granite upland capped by tors. Yet between these two major elements of the Devon scene lies a

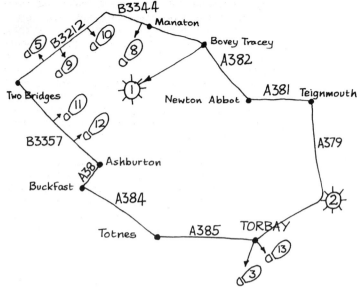

Drive 2

region where rivers cascade down rock-strewn beds cutting deep valleys whose heavily wooded slopes add yet further variety to the landscape.

The drive

Allow a full day for this drive because of the wealth of interesting places along the route. To see the moorland section at its best, choose a sunny day.

Begin at Torquay
🚻 M WC 🅿️ 🅿️
🏰 ∅ 🍴 🍽️

Leave on the coast road (Marine Drive) then via Babbacombe to Teignmouth (A379). Do not take the main Babbacombe road

Torquay lies at the northern end of Torbay, and its palm-lined streets are contoured up the steep limestone hills to provide sweeping views over the bay. There are few signs now of the original fishing village from which developed one of Britain's most popular resorts, and even the headland has been completely overwhelmed by building. However, the coast road is less developed and provides an opportunity to look across to Berry Head, a similar limestone headland at the southern end of Torbay. Yet although the rock is mainly limestone, there is actually a mix of many bands of rock, some tough, others weak (see View 1), whose different resistances to wave action produce an intricately crenulate coast.

From Babbacombe the road is forced over half a mile (1 km) inland by short, steep-sided valleys that fret the cliffs. Here the rock is no longer the dove-grey limestone but the rich red shales and sand-stones that are more characteristic of Devon rocks.

Teignmouth is partly an industrial town, partly a holiday resort. The docks lie in the natural shelter provided by a sand ridge that juts out from the north shore and more than half closes the river estuary. It also forces river water to wash against the north shore, keeping deep water by the docks. The sand to make this ridge comes mainly from the cliffs near Dawlish and shows how the sea compensates for eroding one part of the coast by depositing material elsewhere.

Teignmouth's fishing-port origins lie near the granite-built quayside, where there is still a maze of narrow streets whose form dates back to the Middle Ages and which are a stark contrast to the broader streets and hotel-lined promenades along the coast. As at Torquay, the main holiday trade began soon after the railway arrived, but the imposing Regency-style seafront terraces are a reflection of the well-to-do people who were the first holiday-makers in Teignmouth in the era before the iron road brought a massive influx of visitors.

Whereas Teignmouth owes its growth to the harbour, Newton Abbot, lying at the head of the Teign estuary, has grown at the point where the river could readily be crossed. The Teign estuary, in common with the other wide estuaries of the South Devon coast, keeps the main lines of communication well inland and, with the exception of Torbay, all the large urban centres lie at a distance from the sea.

Newton Abbot has very ancient origins. It was established by Torre Abbey (hence 'new town of the abbey') in the 12th century. However, all medieval traces were swept away as the town grew in the 19th century to become the hub of the railway and road network for South Devon. The town lies squarely on the eastern part of the South Hams peninsula, that broad area of plateau land lying to the south of Dartmoor. The plateau has been cut up into a rectangular pattern of hills and valleys by streams draining from the moors, and this forces most roads to follow either upland or lowland routes. The road to Bovey Tracey begins near to the River Teign, paralleling an earlier choice by both canal and railway engineers who needed to provide a link to clay pits near Bovey (the clay pits lie on the left-hand side of the road).

Bovey Tracey lies on the eastern side of the River Bovey on land just above flood level. On the

At Teignmouth
🅸 WC 🅿0 🅿
🚻 ∅ 🚻 🅯
Take A381 [Newton Abbot >]

At Newton Abbot
WC 🅿0 🅿 🚻 ∅
🚻 🅯
Take A382 [Bovey Tracey >]

On approaching Bovey Tracey turn left B3344 [Manaton >]

western side lies a small settlement also on dry land, located at the place where the lowland route crosses the river and joins with the road to the moors.

This leads you to a starkly different landscape. At first following just above the Bovey, the rapidly steepening valley sides soon force the road ever higher on to the shoulder of the moors. The abrupt change in landscapes signifies the end of the soft shales and sandstone, which have been eroded to lowland, and the start of tougher granite. As rivers tumble from the granite, they cut deep trenches in the moor edge, effectively preventing their use by any form of road.

Walk 8 at Manaton

As far as Manaton there is a great contrast between left- and right-hand sides of the road, with wide views over the lowland plain to the right, and the broad backs of the tor-capped moors to the left. Here you can see very clearly the effect of the forces of erosion at work on soft and hard rock in helping to form the variety of the countryside. The moorland is a harsh place for gaining a living and all settlements take full advantage of any shelter provided by river valleys. But notice how shallow are the valleys in this tough rock.

Manaton is little more than a hamlet strung out on a shoulder of land between moor and valley. Indeed, nearby Widecombe (made famous by the fair that has been held there since Norman times on the second Tuesday in September) is the main settlement of an 11 000 acre parish that houses less than 400 people.

The open landscape of the moor, with its poor quality grasses that offer little opportunity for anything other than sheep and pony grazing, provides

In 11 miles (18 km) at T-junction with B3212 turn left [Postbridge >] (first left Walks 10, 11; Walk 5 at Postbridge)

a type of countryside unique in Britain. It is best seen in late summer when the flowering heather turns this wild and lovely country into a land of pinks and purples.

Although the moors now seem to offer little to man, they have been of considerable importance in the past. Ancient peoples used these moors extensively, both for grazing and for cultivation. The many stove rows, burial chambers and the corral at Grimspound all bear silent witness to a time when the landscape was tree-clad and more sheltered.

More than two millennia later, when England was threatened by attack from the Spaniards, the

(Opposite) **A modern apartment block in Meadfoot Bay provides a harsh contrast to the forest-clad headland**

vantage point offered by the moors enabled beacon fires to be seen far off. Hameldown Beacon, which forms the highest moorland to the left of the road, derives its name from this important period in English history.

For many centuries the moors again proved valuable, both for minerals (tin, copper, zinc) and as a source of stone. In fact many of the sheltered parking areas beside the road are provided by small quarries where weathered granite (called growan) has been carried away to make the surface for roads. Most famous of all is the granite quarried for building stone from the much larger pits, often hundreds of feet deep (see Haytor Rocks, View 1).

Postbridge
🅿 **WC** 🚻 PO ♿ 🍴

Until the 18th century, the cross-moor roads were nothing better than wide, muddy, rutted tracks, used mostly by farmers driving their animals to market. The rudimentary granite-slab clapper bridge at Postbridge dates from this early period. The present road alignment does not follow the old drove road very closely, however, except at river crossings, for good footings on both banks are rare. Most settlements, such as Postbridge, were founded in the 18th century when turnpike roads were built for post coaches, and acted as stations for changing horses.

At Two Bridges Hotel turn left B3357 [Ashburton >]

Dartmeet 🅿 ♿ **WC**
Walk 11

Beyond Dartmeet (again the site of a clapper bridge) the East and West Dart combine to give a substantial river, which cuts deeply into the moor edge. As with the Bovey valley, this section of the Dart is too steep-sided to be followed by the road, which maintains a high-level route. At New Bridge the excessively tortuous path of the Dart brings road and river together again as the road is taken across the neck of a wide meander. Then the road cuts away from the river again and emerges on the lower ground of South Hams.

New Bridge
🅿 ℹ **WC**
Walk 12

Buckfastleigh lies on the moor edge, a small market town beside the much smaller but more famous hamlet of Buckfast with its Cistercian abbey. Although it lies on the main moor-edge route, it is not a good site for trade and Buckfast-leigh has never been able to compete with nearby Totnes, which lies full square amid the agricultural lands of the plateau. Totnes occupies a situation exactly parallel with that of Newton Abbot, this time at the head of the River Dart. However, the site of Totnes is one of the most commanding and

Join A38 dual carriageway southbound [Plymouth >] and exit at next junction A384 [Totnes >]

At Totnes (town guide on Drive 1) take A385 [Torbay (Paignton) >]

(Opposite) **The East Gate of Totnes**

attractive in South Devon. Ancient Totnes was founded by the Saxons on the isolated hill that overlooks the river. When the Normans arrived, they built a castle on the hill and a town wall to enclose the settlement that grew beside the castle gate. The town still retains many fine medieval buildings and substantial lengths of wall from the age when it prospered on the wool trade. Today it is a thriving market town but heavily dependent on the holiday-makers who visit it while staying at nearby Torbay.

3 The northern moor and western valleys

Introduction
The northern and western moor is the most isolated part of Dartmoor. It catches the full force of the northwesterly gales in winter, receives the highest rainfall, and has the poorest grazing land. To the west lies the River Tamar and its tributaries, which cut gashes across the landscape so deep they almost sever Cornwall from Devon. For centuries

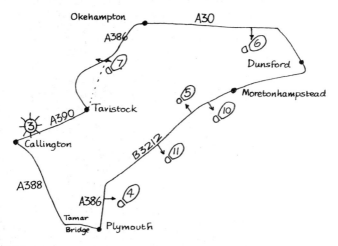

Drive 3

the moor and river barriers have severely restricted the movements of people: the Tamar could only be bridged south of Gunnislake – more than 20 miles (32 km) inland from the coast; the moor could not be crossed and routes were forced to diverge by up to 25 miles (40 km). The area to the west of the moor remained an isolated and backward pocket of England that developed little until the present century.

(Opposite) **The engine house of Wheal Betsy (now preserved by the National Trust) lies above extensive spoil heaps that are at last being cloaked in vegetation; the typical tor-capped moorland profile forms the backdrop to the scene.**

Although the western and northern moors were so isolated, men struggled to overcome the difficulties of the landscape in their search for the mineral riches – tin, copper and even gold and silver – exposed by the swiftly flowing rivers. For most of its time the land has therefore been one of extreme contrast; lonely bleak moor and plateau for the most part, yet dotted with small sites of great activity, noise and bustle wherever minerals were to be found.

The first part of the drive takes us out of Plymouth and on to the cross-moor road via the isolated prison village of Princetown. Beyond the headwater valleys of the River Dart (after which the moor road is named) the route descends to the deeply trenched valley of the River Teign, and then on the moorland shoulder through Okehampton to the equally dramatic western valleys.

The drive

From Plymouth
A386 [Tavistock >]

(At Roborough,
Walk 4
[Bickleigh >])

At Yelverton
🅿 WC 🚻 🅿🅾 ⊘ 🍴
Take B3212
[Princetown >]

Cut off from the western side of the Tamar estuary, Plymouth has extended drab grey tentacles of suburbia far on to the eastern hills. However, beyond Plymouth Airport the land rises quickly to gain the shoulder of the moor, and heather replaces houses and gardens. Here the main road follows a straight ridge-top course running parallel to two south-trending valleys; on the left is the River Tavy, on the right the River Plym, each trenched in a deep, forest-clad defile. This ridge provides a natural ramp up to the moor edge. At its summit lies the small town of Yelverton, surrounded on three sides by valleys and occupying a neck of higher land that provides the gateway to the moor.

Eastwards from Yelverton lies the high moor, signalled immediately ahead by the prominent hill of Sharpitor (1312 ft; 400 m) with its frost-riven crown of massive tor stones. Now with tors to the left and right, the route picks its way among the moortop hills and valleys, skirting the highest tors and avoiding the deepest bogs. Only the sheep and the famous Dartmoor ponies can survive the harsh climate and poor quality grasses of the moor top, and even they need a helping hand in many winters. However, despite its open solitude, the moor provides one of England's largest areas of heather – a dull-green carpet for much of the year but a glorious rich purple in August and September, a crowning glory to this the most wild landscape in southern Britain.

The wildness of the landscape is one of the main reasons for the location of Dartmoor's famous prison at Princetown, built originally by French prisoners during the Napoleonic wars nearly two centuries ago. But the village, which stands in a dry saddle of land between tors, was designed to be far more important than the home of a prison, as its name suggests. Sir Thomas Tyrwhitt, who was Lord Warden of the Stannaries in the 18th century, decided to improve the moor and build a town where the two moor roads crossed. The land was given by the Prince of Wales (hence Princetown). The chances of development on an exposed site with over 80 in (2030 mm) of rain each year were, however, never good and, besides the prison, extensive granite quarrying was the only successful venture. Even the modern use of the high site for a television station (North Hessory Tor, 1695 ft; 517 m) is achieved with few personnel.

Two Bridges ⊟
B3212 [Moreton-
hampstead >]

The road beyond Princetown and Two Bridges dates back to medieval times, its heritage marked by the old clapper bridges, the most famous of which is at Postbridge. These bridges allowed travellers to get across the moor as quickly as possible and they reflect how Dartmoor's harsh climate has been feared for many generations. Even today there is no more settlement than the occasional lonely inn or farmhouse. Paradoxically, however, everywhere around lie the standing stones, circles and burial chambers of the Stone and Bronze Age peoples who sought the moor in preference to the encircling lowland. As you speed across the moorland, reflect on the landscape your ancestors found – a land clothed in oak forest out of which they had to hack clearings. The barren moorland you see is the result of thousands of years of tree felling and sheep grazing, its peat bogs and acid soils a stark reminder of a farming system that ruined for ever a fertile hill land.

Walks 11, 12
turn right B3357

Postbridge, Walk 5

The stone crosses lining the moorland route are also a reminder of the ancient origins of the road: they are the medieval equivalent of route signs. The last of these crosses lies at the junction with the road to Bovey Tracey (B3344) and marks the end of the moor. Beyond lies the lower, more sheltered land surrounding Moretonhampstead (*mor* means 'by a fen'; *ton* means 'settlement').

2 miles (3 km)
beyond Warren
House Inn,
turn right
[Widecombe >],
Walks 8, 9, 10

Moretonhampstead is a market town nestling between steep-sided valleys, which have trenched into the softer rocks that ring the moor. It was developed on a saddle of land that separates streams flowing north to the River Teign from those flowing south to the River Bovey. The saddle provides nearly the last piece of the ramp that lowers the road gently to the eastern lowlands, and beyond lies only one more ridge.

Moretonhampstead
P WC ⊟ 🏠 ➹ PI ∅
Take B3212
[Exeter >]

As you rise up the hillside to Mardon Down,

The northern moor and western valleys ⟍ 61

Turn left
[Dunsford >].
In village
straight on
[Cheriton Bishops >].
At A30 turn left
[Okehampton >]

Okehampton 🅿 **WC**
🚻 ⛽ 🅿 Ⓟ ⊘ 🏨 ⓘ

From Okehampton
A30, then fork left
A386 [Tavistock >].
In 5 miles (8 km), at
Dartmoor Inn, turn
right [Lydford >]

Lydford 🏨 (NT) 🚻
⛽ 🅿 ⊘ 🏨 **WC**
[Brent Tor >] then
[Tavistock >]

there is a last glimpse of Dartmoor, for on the other side the road descends swiftly to the Teign valley and its wooded slopes. Dunsford is a village of the plain, a huddle of pretty thatched cottages set around a stone-built church on the side of the valley, just out of reach of the river floods. Here, too, the contrast between moor and lowland is displayed: the narrow lanes are sunk deep between high earth and stone-built banks rather than un-fenced as on the moor. Farming, too, is quite different, the sheep ranging being replaced with dairy farming on rich pastureland. This is a pattern that continues as far as Okehampton, a site chosen for its classic strategic advantages.

The present settlement of Okehampton was built on a wedge-shaped site between two branches of the Okemont river a mile from the castle. The castle commands the whole east–west valley route around the moor edge, a strong site made even stronger by an artificial cut on the western side. It was a strategic site that was later to prove a trading advantage, for Okehampton is now the chief market town of the northern moor. The main road to Plymouth skirts the shoulder of the moor from Okehampton Castle, rising for only a few miles to cross the outlying ridge of moorland called Black Down (1035 ft; 315 m). Both ends of the road across Black Down are marked by inns: Dart-moor Inn to the north and Blackdown Inn at Mary Tavy in the south. However, for many centuries the road connecting Okehampton with Tavistock avoided Black Down and veered westwards at Dartmoor Inn, first to Lydford then, keeping away from the deeply trenched valley of the River Lyd (Walk 7), it followed the marshy floor of the River Burn, and passed the isolated pinnacle of Brent Tor before heading directly south to Tavistock.

Brent Tor (possibly from *brent* meaning 'steep') is one of the few remanent volcanoes to be found on the moor: a place where molten rock once reached the surface to eject great clouds of ash much as Mount St Helens has done in recent years. Brent Tor is the remains of lava which, on cooling, finally plugged the volcano and sealed it for ever. It makes an ideal vantage point, with views stretching west across Kit Hill to the plateau lands of Cornwall, but is a most unlikely place for the church that crowns its rocky top. St Michael of the Rock 'full bleak, and

(Opposite) **The charming village of Dunsford is built just above the marshy ground of the Teign floodplain**

weather beaten, all alone, as it were forsaken' was built about 1130, the fourth smallest complete parish church in England, being only 37 ft (11.2 m) long and 14 ft 6 in (4.4 m) wide and able to seat about 50 people if they have the energy to climb the hill on the summer evenings when services are held. This church is full of mystery: why was it built here on the open moor; why was it important enough to have a market charter and a three-day Michaelmas fair in the Middle Ages? The reasons are now lost in history, along with any trace of the Iron Age people who, over a thousand years earlier, had enclosed the tor with a circular earthen bank.

Tavistock **P 🛉 M**
🍽 🐾 ⌀ 🅿️ WC
Take A390
[Callington >]

Tavistock, like Lydford, was a Stannary Town, a place where tin, mined from the moors, had to be stamped and weighed. However, Tavistock is by far the younger town, being founded by the monks of Tavistock Abbey in about 1105 to cash in on the trade that tin mining was bringing to the area of west Dartmoor. As it turned out, the site of Tavistock, in a sheltered but accessible valley, was more favourable than Lydford. Gradually, Tavistock usurped Lydford's trade and left it as an isolated moor-edge hamlet. In Tavistock, only isolated fragments of the Abbey remain to show where the old town was first established below a hill and on the narrow north bank of the River Tavy. Indeed, the prosperity brought by copper mining in the 18th century and the railway in the 19th led to an expansion that has almost obliterated the signs of Tavistock's early history. So great was the demand for housing in the 19th century that a planned estate was laid out on the Plymouth road and many roads in the centre were widened and remodelled. Today only the streets beside the Market Square retain a medieval plan.

The road between Tavistock and Kit Hill is dominated by the steep wooded valleys cut by the River Tamar and its tributaries as they plunge southwards to the sea. This is a landscape that posed many problems for the road builder but more particularly for the mine owners, because they had to export heavy and bulky ore.

Most people associate mining in Devon and Cornwall with tin, yet many of the major mines in the Tavistock area were worked for copper. Tin was mined very early in the history of the area and had been worked out by the late Middle Ages. It was the

(Opposite) **St Michael's church, Brent Tor**

discovery of copper in the age of steam that led to the construction of canals, railways, mine engines and all the paraphernalia of industrialisation. In the 50 years from 1850 a great copper boom overtook the area. The greatest mine of all – the Devon Great Consoles – lay on the hill west of Tavistock, almost overlooking the Tamar Gorge. To export the ore it was necessary to dig a canal from the mine through a hillside just to gain the valley side. Even so, the canal emerged high above the river and the ore had to be carried down an inclined plane on trucks before it could reach the riverside port of Morwellham. Morwellham, until recently little more than an overgrown ruin, has now been reconstructed and provides a fascinating glimpse back to the time when industry dominated the valley. Elsewhere, on all the nearby hilltops, the stark silhouettes of the mine engine houses look on mournfully.

West of Gunnislake, granite rises to the surface once more, carrying the road high above the southern plateau and providing an opportunity to look down on the coastal regions of South Devon and Cornwall, to see how the steep-sided, heavily wooded valleys isolate each ridge of land from its neighbour. In the distance lie the shimmering waters of the Tamar estuary and the outskirts of Plymouth. However, until the construction of the Tamar Bridge, Plymouth could only be reached by a long detour via Tavistock, or by ferry. It is for this reason that the countryside between Callington and Plymouth shows none of the suburban and commuter village development so characteristic of the eastern Tamar.

The land stretching to either side of the River Tamar is remarkably level, varying little from 450 to 500 ft (137 to 152 m) in height. Yet beneath the heavy clay soils lie rocks of considerable variety. Here we see part of South Devon's most recent history, a period during which the land rose from the sea leaving what was once the level sea bed now over 400 ft (122 m) above the present sea. In terms of landscape formation this has happened so quickly (over perhaps less than a million years) that the rivers have only been able to keep pace with the rising land by cutting deep trenches.

Changes in the relative heights of land and sea are very important to South Devon, producing the two major features of plateau and deeply gorged valleys. The most recent change of sea level has been upwards, when the sea spilled into, and flooded, the lower part of the Tamar valley towards

(In 2 miles (3 km) turn left [Morwellham Quay >])

Callington
P WC ♿ ⛽ 🛏 P0 Ø
Take A388
[Plymouth >] via
Tamar Bridge

the close of the Ice Age, when ice melted and the meltwater returned to the sea.

Plymouth and Devonport largely owe their prosperity to the sheltered deep waters created by the recent rise in sea level. However, the Tamar is already filling the estuary with silt eroded from the moors. Now, it can provide anchorage for aircraft carriers but within a few more centuries it will have silted up completely. Look up stream as you cross the Tamar Bridge. At low tide you can already see wide mud banks lining both shores, telltale signs that the landscape is continually changing.

KESTREL

This is the most frequently seen falcon in Britain, a bird of prey that hovers high above the ground before swooping down to catch voles and other small mammals from open grassland or moor. The kestrel is a beautiful chestnut colour, and the male bird has a blue–grey head and tail.

The northern moor and western valleys 67

Walks of moor, valley and coast

1 The threatening rocks: Bolt Head

Introduction

Tucked away on the southernmost headland of Devon and isolated from through-roads by the long estuaries of the Avon and Kingsbridge lies the small town of Salcombe. Deriving its name of 'salt valley' from the time when salt was evaporated from sea water by heating it in large pans on the beach, it became a small seaport and attracted a few holiday villas in the 19th century. Today it remains a quiet backwater in this busy part of Britain, a centre for yachts and for those who like to follow a cliff path to Bolt Head that must give one of the finest scenic walks in the country. Here you will find imposing craggy cliffs, and views over sheltered harbours, together with sandy, pocket beaches, wooded valleys and even palm trees, and all along an even and easy path.

Salcombe lies south of Kingsbridge on A381. At Salcombe turn right [South Sands, North Sands, Bolt Head >]. **P** at North Sands at foot of switchback road. Limited **P** at South Sands and at Sharp Tor House (NT)

The walks

Both walks are easy.

(a) From grounds of National Trust Sharp Tor House to Bolt Head along coast path and return. Follow **2,3,4,2** (1½ hours).

(b) From North Sands to visit beaches, Bolt Head, return along cliff-top and visit National Trust gardens. Follow **1,2,3,4,5,1** (half a day).

The route

The rocks that form the impressive scenery of Bolt Head are not the typical red Devon rocks but highly contorted grey and green slates, which have been stood on edge in such a way that each rock band now projects straight out to sea. Tough rocks make the headlands that separate the bays of

1 Follow the road to the NT entrance

North Sands from South Sands and provide the foundation for Fort Charles and the remains of Salcombe Castle. In contrast, the weaker rocks have been washed away by the sea to form deep coves, and by streams that flow swiftly from the plateau top to create deep, steep-sided valleys.

The bands of tough rock have been partly responsible for Salcombe's unsuitability as a major harbour, because they make a rocky threshold that extends from one side of the estuary to the other. Nevertheless, in the time of Henry VIII, the harbour was sufficiently important to warrant the

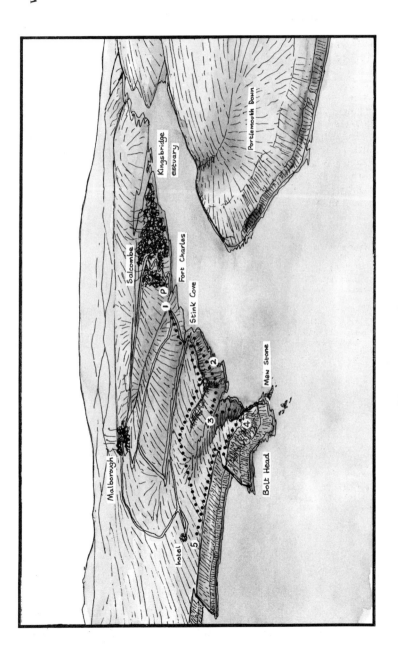

replacement of the ruined castle with Fort Charles as a defence against possible attack by the French.

The narrow road from the car park rises and falls between the pocket bays, each beach the end of a small infilled river valley. This is a beautiful walk shaded by broadleaved and coniferous trees and with views to the azure blue waters of the estuary. Here, too, ivy and many small plants of the woodland floor occur at eye level, growing on the soil above the walled sides of the road.

As you leave South Sands the view begins to widen into broad vistas over the lower estuary, but even this is no preparation for the dramatic scenery about to unfold ahead, beyond the honeysuckle-clad glade entrance to the National Trust land. After the woodland, the grassy headland comes into view. Above, like a line of camouflaged rockets 2 waiting to be fired on some unsuspecting target in the bay, is a row of tough blue–grey rocks that dominate much of Bolt Head. These are the jagged remnants of rocks baked and contorted nearly 300 million years ago when Devon was part of a mountain range. Deeply buried for so long, only now when the mountains have become levelled have they been exposed at the surface.

The path cuts right through more razor-shaped rocks, at one point even going into a small tunnel. Pick up one of the shiny slivers of rock and try to scratch or break it – a difficult task that helps one to understand why Bolt Head still projects outwards to the sea so prominently.

3 Stairhole Cove, beyond the 'rocket' cliff, has been etched out of a band of weaker rocks by a small stream that rises on the plateau above. Beyond it lies the promontory of Bolt Head, its more gentle grass-covered upper slope still at the angle formed during the Ice Age, when the slope was part of a valley stretching far out into the English Channel. By contrast the lower slope is nearly vertical and shows how far the winter waves have cut into the slope since the Ice Age departed 12 000 years ago. Constant wave action has also etched out Stairhole Cove, cutting back into a small valley so far that a waterfall has been formed.

The top of the cliff forms the southern edge of the South Hams plateau. It looks just as though someone had taken a knife and sliced the top cleanly away. This is the old sea floor, now lifted over

(Opposite) **North Sands, Salcombe, with the tough rock bar on which the ruins of the castle lie.**

200 ft (60 m) clear of the water, the distant hills
4 marking the line of the long-abandoned cliffs.

From the lookout post you have a view south-
west across the wide ocean: there is no land this
way before South America! In the same direction
you can see the (apparently) tiny needle of the
Eddystone Lighthouse astride one of the oldest
rock reefs in Britain. With binoculars you can even
see the stump of the old ruined lighthouse to the
right of the new one. The distant land is the
southern outpost of Cornwall and the Lizard Head.
The lookout post provides almost a seagull's-eye
view of the nearby coast, with its headlands and
coves, its steeply dipping rocks, its cliffs and rocky
ledges. From here the flatness of the plateau is all
the more striking. The plateau and the rocky ledge
that skirts the cliff foot have much in common for,
given time, the cliff will be worn back and the ledge
will become a wide platform which, like the plateau
we see today, may also eventually be lifted up
by forces within the Earth to form another new
cliff-top.

Follow the coast path
to the hotel, 5, or cut
across the headland,
following the clifftop
footpath to the road

2   The last foothold on England: Start Point

Introduction
Start Point is one of the southernmost outposts of Devon. The red–
brown rocks so characteristic of the rest of the county are left behind
and instead there are contorted and baked rocks set out in band after
band of green and purple, some standing on end, others bent over
into intricately folded patterns, and all etched by the sea into a maze
of tiny coves.

The sea can be especially powerful at Start Point and the exposed
west-facing shore is uninhabited. Even on the sheltered east, only
tiny hamlets survive in an area that has no natural harbour. Nevertheless, people here have had more to fear from the hand of man than
Nature, with the result that the hamlet of Hallsands has all but
disappeared into the sea.

From Kingsbridge
take A379
[Dartmouth >].
At Stokenham [Start
Point >]. 🅿 on cliff
above lighthouse.

The walks
(a) Short and easy to visit the coastal coves and
     lighthouse of Start Point. Follow **1,2,3,1** (1½
     hours).
(b) Longer, entirely on gentle grade footpaths to
     include the ruins of Hallsands. Follow **1,2,3,1,
     4,5,1** (half a day).

(Opposite) **The towering pinnacles of rock above the path on Bolt Head**

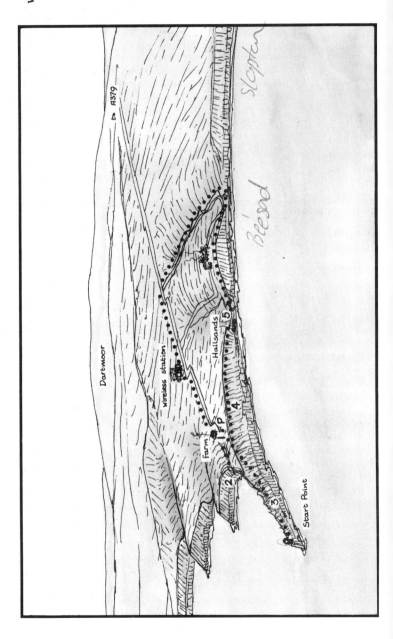

The route

1

From 🅿 walk
towards lighthouse
and through gate.
Turn right and
follow track to Start
Farm and sea

The Start headland shows dramatically how the respective effects of rivers and the sea on the rocks produce completely contrasting types of landscape. Look across the gently rolling countryside of South Hams from the car park and you gain an impression of uniformity, of an unvarying rock etched by a number of small streams to give a pattern of steep-sided valleys. Now look down to the cliffs below, where a fretted coastline of headlands and bays, rocky platforms and beaches reveals the true pattern of rocks of great complexity.

Waves reveal contrasts in rocks more readily than rivers because each band of rock is directly attacked by the waves and its broken fragments are immediately washed away. Weathered material on land, however, must be carried over long slopes before it can be removed by running water. On land, therefore, slopes have to be adjusted to carry material from hard and soft rocks alike: there must be even slopes leading from the highest ridge to the stream bank. There is no place for upstanding ridges or deep trenches there: soil would simply bank up against a ridge until it became overwhelmed, or fill in a trench until it ceased to exist.

It has never been easy to gain a living from the exposed headlands of the South Devon coast. Where otherwise the flat-topped cliffs and deep soils provide rich farmland, the headlands take the full force of the strong salt-laden winds and only pasture flourishes. Indeed, both shelter and fresh water are scarce commodities at Start Point; where they occur together lies the only farm on the headland, and even this huddles behind the shelter of trees.

A walk along this path on a fine summer's day makes it very difficult to appreciate the exposed and wind-blown nature of the area in winter. But picture a walk along the same path in January with a gale blowing in from the Atlantic and the wind driving horizontally across the hedge tops and you will understand why the farm buildings are gathered in a bend in a part of the valley that faces away from the open sea, turning their backs as far as possible on Nature at her worst.

Behind the farm stands a BBC radio transmitting station, fully exposed to the gales. It is a reminder of the differences between new and old. When the farmhouse was built it sought a location in harmony with the environment, sheltering in the valley and with a secure water supply. When the radio station arrived it was sited with a clear prospect where radio waves could not be distorted by nearby hills. Mains water and electricity make this exposed site feasible, although possibly some would regard its intrusion as being at the expense of the countryside.

2 Exposed though this headland is today, a few tens of thousands of years ago conditions were immeasurably worse. At that time, during the Ice Age, the vegetation had died and soil had slipped over the cliffs, exposing the weak slate rock below. Here, frost cracked the rocks and sent flakes cascading down the hillside to build up like some vast spoil heap. This was the time when the rugged outline of the headland spine was formed, and its gaunt profile is all that remains after millennia of attack, the bulk of its material now littering the slopes at its feet. Much of this material is covered by grass and soil once again, but it is still clearly revealed at the coast, where it makes the entire undercliff. When even tough rocks cannot resist the sea, this accumulation of flakes stands little chance of remaining for long, and already it has been washed away from a broad width of coast, its remnants standing out to sea like a row of old men, exposing the former rock ledge on which it was built.

3 Rocks do not display their weaknesses readily and although the fretted coast leading to the lighthouse shows how wave action has found weaknesses by the score, the nature of each weakness remains concealed. But any rock so heavily contorted by massive forces long ago must surely have many defects in its armour, as can more clearly be seen near Hallsands.

Return to 🅿 and follow footpath diagonally down cliff to Hallsands hamlet

The cliff between the car park and the hamlet of Hallsands is called a hogsback cliff, meaning it has an upper, more gentle slope terminated below in a vertical drop to the sea. Such cliffs are widespread in the South-West and, like the coast beside Start Farm, are the result of a long period of frost shattering during the Ice Age, the upper slope being reduced to such an angle that frost-riven debris could just slide over it and expose new rock. Since this time, waves have attacked and steepened the lower part of the cliff once more and continue actively to make further inroads, as landslides reveal.

Dramatic although these natural changes have been, none can match the speed with which man has inadvertently altered the coast near Hallsands.

SESSILE OAK

Taller and more upright than its low-land relative, the sessile oak is a native of west and northern Britain, occurring widely on slightly acid soils and on hills. It has larger, more leathery and well formed leaves than the Common Oak, but the chief means of distinguishing between species lies in the acorns: sessile means stalkless, and the acorns are held in groups tightly to the twigs.

(120 ft; 40 m)

OYSTERCATCHER

The smart, black and white oystercatcher has a very distinctive long orange bill, which it uses to pierce the shells of the mussels on which it feeds. You will see it on most rocky foreshores where mussels, limpets or crabs can be found in tidal pools. In flight, oystercatchers can be identified by white bars that run along both wings.

At the cliff-top there are a few cottages, some precariously near the edge; a little further on, a barn hangs half over the cliff, and beyond that the road and a complete row of houses have already gone. But the most spectacular results lie down near the water, for here, less than a century ago, the fishermen of Hallsands used to draw their boats up on to the beach that lay between the sea and their little houses. Today only a few walls remain to mark the tragedy that befell the community soon after dredging for shingle began off shore. Over half a million tons of shingle were taken to build nearby Devonport Dockyard, half a million tons that had been protecting Hallsands from the sea. In just a few years the beach level dropped over 15 ft (4.5 m) and the sea was able to rush in and attack the rocky bench on which the houses were built.

As you make your way carefully through the remains of these long-abandoned houses, part of the path leads over a gap beyond a wall. Look down to the right: below you, waves beat against the walls of a cave excavated along a line of shattered rock since the dredging began. At low tide you can go into the cave and look up to the houses: clearly it will not be long before all is lost. Nothing can be done to preserve Hallsands, but the experience of this tragedy can at least act as a warning for those who would exploit one part of Nature without due thought to its consequences.

From Hallsands Hotel follow the road to the plateau then turn left and return to 🅿

3   In the steps of history: the Dart estuary

Introduction
Dartmouth must be one of the best known and yet most inaccessible towns in England. Indeed so tortuous is the journey to Torbay that ferries have long operated across to the village of Kingswear. Here, towards the end of the 19th century, the railway from Torquay terminated, thwarted in its crossing of the Dart by the refusal of local landowners to allow it on their land. The difficulty of bridging the estuary has, however, maintained a useful purpose for Kingswear without which it might have faded away entirely. Today, its main function is to provide a quiet environment for those seeking a home in the country on retirement. Most of the village lies on the steep side of a wooded valley but stretches round into the no less steep slopes overlooking the open sea. From its streets two quite different walks diverge, one out towards the sea, where storm waves have fretted the coast,

🚗 From Torbay take A379 [Dartmouth >]. At Hillhead cross-roads [lower ferry >]. 🅿 on approach road to village or by harbour

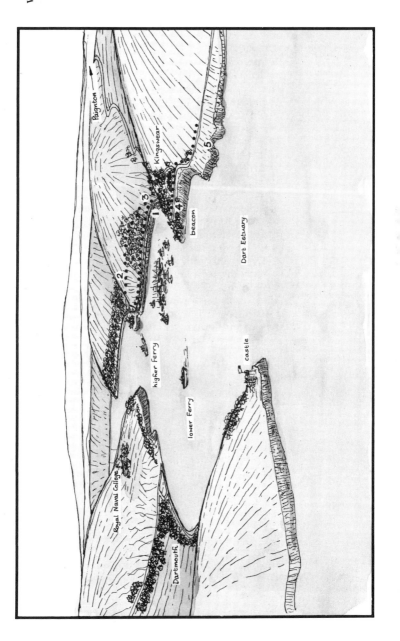

Paignton

Kingswear

3

2

1

4

5

beacon

higher Ferry

lower Ferry

castle

Dart Estuary

Royal Naval College

Dartmouth

the other towards the calm inner harbour opposite the main centre of Dartmouth town.

The walk
Both sections of the walk are short and easy, each taking about an hour.

The route
Inland. The Dart estuary is a ria, a steep-sided valley whose floor was deeply trenched during the Ice Age when the sea level was much lower than today, and was subsequently partly drowned when the sea level returned to normal. Storm waves do not enter the harbour reach and have not been able to cut a cliff at the foot of the slopes; neither have the slopes been able to adjust to their changed situation. As a result the valley sides still plunge quite unnaturally into the water. With such steep sides it was quite a difficult task to accommodate a railway and, for the whole distance between Kingswear and the upper ferry, the track has been laid on an artificial embankment, a causeway whose sweeping curve is in stark contrast to the irregular valley side.

Cross railway by footbridge and follow footpath to higher ferry

1

From the path the position of Dartmouth is very clear, its roads following steep valley routes as they climb from the harbour side to the plateau 500 ft (150 m) above. The lack of flat land by the water side has forced building to sprawl beside the water for over a mile, much of it trapped below the steep valley slope. Only the Royal Naval College occupies a substantial site, set back on the landward side of the town on a prominent spur that allows a sweeping vista down the length of the harbour. Below the college there are still ship repair and building yards, but their importance is greatly reduced from the time when Dartmouth was a major shipbuilding centre for the Navy.

At higher ferry walk ½ mile (0.8 km) up the main road and turn sharp left along a track, then a path to Kingswear

2

The path back to Kingswear follows the upper part of the heavily wooded valley slope, providing a lovely view over the harbour. In contrast to Kingswear, where the shales are grey, the track exposes steeply angled beds of red shale in which the upper harbour valley has been cut, a rock that weathers to give the deep, red soil for which Devon is so renowned. Oak, beech and ash are all present here, providing pleasant shade during a walk on a warm day. The path returns over the hillside and

(Opposite) **A bench in the valley side has been used by the builders of the Royal Naval College, but the harbour is now the home of pleasure yachts rather than naval craft**

descends to the edge of the small muddy harbour crossed by the railway embankment. Built into the shale rockside of this harbour are the remains of white-painted lime kilns, once used to fire a local band of limestone for the making of fertiliser. From this little harbour sailing boats would take their lime to other small ports to be used by those who farmed on poor soils.

3 *Towards the sea.* Building on the steep valley side at Kingswear has always presented problems, and newer houses have had to be constructed on terraces connected by steep flights of steps. Virtually everyone has to walk up and down dozens of

Opposite station go under arch, up steps and seawards then left on road overlooking harbour

A light beacon stands by the wooded slopes where estuary meets the sea and each prominent ledge at water level marks a tough band of rock; the same ledge will also be found across the harbour

steps to get to their front doors. The steps and
4 interconnecting alleyways constantly give new and
interesting angles to the town. High retaining walls
tower above the streets in an effort to keep gardens
and houses on the slopes. By the harbour old
fishermen's houses have been converted into more
luxurious homes, each with a high wall that makes
access to the shore difficult. However, as the paths
lead seawards, running obliquely up across the hill-
slope, you can obtain fine views over the rooftops
to Dartmouth and its houses, which, like those of
Kingswear, have been packed tightly in terraces
above the waterfront.

Although the land at Kingswear is steep, that
further seawards is almost precipitous and renders
building impossible. Even trees can only just cling
to this slope, their roots deeply embedded in the
shale rock for anchorage.

From above the harbour beacon there are wide
views across the harbour and out to sea. Below the
ledges of tough slate rock jutting out from the small
cliff, each one tracing a line across the estuary to its
partner on the far bank: as in many other places in
South Devon, the rock bands, although so heavily
contorted and stood on edge, still maintain an east–
west alignment.

So steep is this hill slope that the road has had to
cut into solid rock, providing an opportunity to see
the pink-coloured slate at close quarters. Despite its
5 thin cover of stony soil, considerable care has been
taken to plant a wide variety of both broadleaved
and coniferous trees, and the sweet smell of the
conifers is wafted in with the sea breeze. Unfortunately, where the soil is thickest, it is least stable,
for here trees have been content to form their roots
within the soil alone. Many have toppled over, and
others have been uprooted by landslides produced
in winter when, after a heavy storm, the saturated
soil burdened with the extra weight of the trees
has slid over the solid rock below. Landslides are
common on all steep slopes and here treeless scars
show only the position of the most recent slides, for
the scars are quickly healed by new soil formation.
However, the instability is a reminder that these
slopes, so recently formed during the Ice Age, are
once again being moulded by both landslides and
undercutting by the waves to a new shape, an
Return by the same example of the continuous process of landscape
route evolution.

4   The shoulders of Dartmoor: Shaugh Prior

Introduction

The rivers that drain the western slopes of Dartmoor are the most powerful of all the moorland streams. The River Plym rises on the rain-washed slopes of Lee Moor, first cutting only a wide shallow valley in the tough granite. However, after Cadover Bridge, the stream begins to tumble off the moor edge and its course steepens, the valley narrows and the Plym enters one of the finest of the moor-edge gorges. Beyond Shaugh Bridge lies the lower land that surrounds the moor and in these weaker rocks the valley widens once more.

The gorge above Shaugh Bridge is a remarkable natural feature, still clothed in oak forest except where precipitous sides do not allow trees even a meagre foothold. Over the ages, people have been quick to take advantage of this countryside. Bronze Age people lived on the cliff-edged promontory that lies between the River Plym and the River Meavy, and Iron Age people built a defensive earthwork on the same spot. Now climbers pit their skills on the famous Dewerstone Rock cliff, and opposite, on the less steep valley side, lie the ruins of a paper mill, a ferro-ceramic mine and a clay drying plant for the moor-top china clay works.

The walks

(a) Short and quite easy, to see Shaugh Bridge and Shaugh Prior village. Follow **1,2,6,1** (2 hours).

(b) Longer, to visit Shaugh Bridge and the moor edge at Cadover Bridge. Follow **1,2,3,4,5,6,1** (half a day).

🚗 From Plymouth take A386 north to Bickleigh, then [Shaugh Prior >]. 🅿 at Shaugh Bridge (NT) in valley bottom before village

The route

1 If you are expecting the industrial workings to be a blight on the countryside, you may be surprised to learn that you have parked in the remains of the workings! Indeed, although the clay drying plant only closed in the 1960s, it has been dismantled so effectively that it is hard to discern the purpose of what remains. For example, the brick arches are all that is left of the clay drying kilns. Across the river, not half a mile away, lies the bed of a dismantled railway, which was used to carry the dried clay down to Plymouth for export.

Follow the footpath up hill beside the kilns

Today the industrial works are an insignificant part of the Shaugh Bridge scene. Much more impressive is the River Plym as it tumbles over and between the large granite boulders that choke its bed. This is an ancient scene, the lichen-hung trees (still showing signs of coppicing) casting dark shadows, cloaking the valley sides and closing in over the river.

2 🌿   From the steep slope to the moor-edge village of

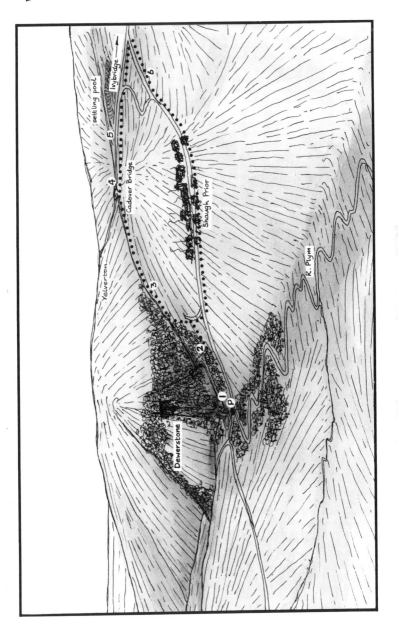

Shaugh Prior there are good views of the 170 ft (52 m) Dewerstone rock, the highest inland granite cliff in Devon. Underfoot the valley side is littered with boulders shed by the upper slopes during the coldest phase of the Ice Age. Today these lichen-covered boulders have been stabilised by the woodland and must now be weathered where they lie.

On reaching a stile and gravel road turn left and follow the road, then footpath parallel to the river

The path runs along the contour of the valley keeping somewhat above the river, constantly in shady woods. It is known as Pipe Track from the time when china clay was washed down through a pipe laid along this course from the clay pits near Cadover Bridge to the drying kilns at Shaugh Bridge.

3   Granite boulders have choked the stream channel at Shaugh Bridge because the gradient is too gentle to allow the water to carry them away. However, on the steep section of the gorge it has been able to keep its bed clear. Indeed, the continual wearing away by gravel and boulders as they are whisked through the channel has produced fluted and pitted shapes. Some of these are deep, circular pools called pot-holes, worn away by small pebbles incessantly being whirled around by eddies in the stream flow.

4   As the path approaches Cadover Bridge, the shoulder of the moor is reached and the stream once more follows a gentle path, its waters having cut no more than a shallow valley into the tough granite. Cadover Bridge lies on a medieval route that crossed the open moor. On the hilltop beyond is a stone cross; there is another on your route to Shaugh Prior. At first they seem strangely sited and with little purpose, but imagine how difficult it must have been to find your way across a feature-less moor before there were roads. The crosses are the medieval equivalent of road signs, showing the way to the safety of the lowland.

The most dominant feature at Cadover Bridge is the large spoil heap of waste from the nearby china clay works. China clay is derived from feldspar, the mineral that makes the rectangular, opaque pink and white crystals that show so prominently in granite. The quarryman's problem, however, is what to do with the rest of the granite. This is a form of quartz sand, which is too expensive to transport away to use as building material and cannot be dumped back whence it came for many of the pits are not yet even half worked out. At present, there-

(Opposite) The boulder-choked channel of the River Plym at Shaugh Bridge

fore, it continues to be piled on to the moor, transforming the bleak heather countryside into one more reminiscent of the moon. However, before you consider these piles of waste to be mere blights on the countryside, look at the pits and spoil heaps beyond the bridge which, having gone out of use, have been graded and landscaped and are gradually regaining a cover of grass.

5   Up stream of Cadover Bridge are other signs of industrial activity. Here, tin was collected by streaming, washing the gravels with stream water, and then dumping the waste in small heaps that

Follow the road south (towards Ivybridge) now litter the valley floor. However, here too you will find a number of flat granite slabs arranged in the form of a primitive bridge. This type of structure is one of the most widespread forms of early bridge, but these are not placed just anywhere across a stream: they need firm foundations on both banks. Thus their sites are chosen with care. A stone bridge was never used at Cadover Bridge because the stream is wide and shallow and could be forded with ease. The bridge dates only from the time of the coming of motorised transport.

6 ✻   Shaugh Prior has grown up in the lee of the moor and offers a marvellous prospect over the Tamar estuary and Plymouth. This hamlet has remained small despite the nearby claypits, for its people are not involved in clay mining but still turn to farming

Go through Shaugh Prior village to 🅿 at bottom of the hill even though this is a region where the land offers little to the farmer.

5   In the miners' footsteps: Postbridge

Introduction

The high moor has always been difficult to cross. In winter, routes that avoided the worst of the bogs were hard to find. One such route connected the moor-edge towns of Chagford in the north-east with Tavistock in the west. This was not a surfaced road, simply a post-marked trail, wide and rutted and often deep with mud. The main obstacles along the way were rivers, particularly the East Dart, and to provide a satisfactory crossing, huge flat slabs of granite were pulled from the nearby tors and built up into a rough structure called a clapper bridge. There are many such bridges on the moor, nearly all of medieval date, the largest of which is at Postbridge. Later, when a turnpike road was built between Tavistock and Moretonhampstead, the clapper bridge (being unsuitable for carriages) was bypassed and a new bridge was built beside it. The present road follows the line of the 18th century turnpike.

Postbridge was used as a toll station along the turnpike, and an inn

(Opposite) **The moorland edge at Cadover Bridge**

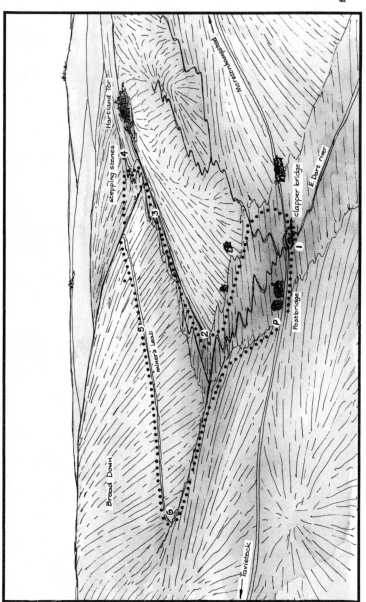

(not the present one) was provided to give some respite to travellers and allow a change of horses. This was also mining country and several large tin mines (including the Vitrifer Mine, Walk 10) were opened near Postbridge, causing the hamlet to grow large enough to warrant the construction of a chapel in the middle of the 19th century. Today the mines have long fallen into ruin but traces of the mining activity on the moor can be seen as you follow the East Dart up stream.

⚑ Postbridge on B3212 Moretonhampstead to Yelverton road

The walk

About 2 hours, a pleasant and easy walk beside the East Dart; however, it can be spongy in places. There are stepping-stones to cross the East Dart but these will be impassable after heavy rain and you will have to retrace your path along the east bank.

The route

1 The clapper bridge

The clapper bridge and nearby boulders that rest by the stream banks are made from granite. This contains crystals of feldspar, mica and quartz, which are more easily recognisable on a pebble taken clean from the water. Search around as you walk up stream and you may find feldspar crystals more than an inch long.

Cross the river and follow [footpath >] beyond bridge to go up stream on right bank. The path follows the wall round the marshy area

The upper valley of the East Dart is very shallow, the river seeming hardly to have cut into the moor at all. In fact the valley has been cut deeper than it looks but, during the Ice Age, when the slopes were bare and granite was prised from the tors by intense frost, not only were the tors exposed but in

2

addition a large amount of material slid down and choked the valley. Thus the Ice Age is responsible for both exposing the tors and filling the valleys. Today the East Dart is still choked with debris and the river flows over a boulder bed rather than over solid rock. Hartland Tor, which overlooks the river, is one obvious source of valley debris, but material would have been supplied from all the nearby slopes.

3 Stone walls of moorland 'improvers'

In the 18th century, people were filled with enthusiasm for land improvement as the agricultural revolution got underway. On Dartmoor, much moorland was enclosed with stone walls by improvers determined to transform the impoverished 'wastes' into productive land. The walls that cross the moor were put up at this time, but there is now little sign of agricultural activity.

(Opposite) **The River Dart flows through a shallow valley cut in solid granite**

Much of the granite is of gravel size and it makes the finer bed material of the stream. Called growan, it is mostly quartz, the most resistant of granite materials. However, the East Dart is not making much impression on moving the boulders, and they still act as useful natural stepping-stones.

4 At confluence, where leat leads from river, use natural stepping-stones

The return route follows an artificial channel whose line will have been clearly seen during the walk up stream. Artificial channels (leats) were cut to carry water for a variety of purposes on the moor:

5 sometimes they were to drive machinery such as crushing hammers in mines or to operate the bellows of a furnace in a blowing house. (There are the ruins of such a blowing house on the low ground below Hartland Tor.) At other times leat water was used to stream tin. The leat cut in the East Dart valley side leads towards the site of an old gunpowder factory located halfway between Two Bridges and Postbridge. Gunpowder was an important tool for both miner and quarryman.

The leat is a newcomer to the moorland scene.

Follow the leat until it is crossed by the drift lane

Much older is the drift lane (which had to be provided with a slab bridge over the leat). Part sheltered between walls of granite, part sunken by long use, this is the track used to bring sheep

6 down off the moors in autumn. Notice how nearby Archerton Farm lies in the fold of the hills, sheltering from the harsh westerly winds of winter. Like many other old settlements, this farm is also situated beside a spring, which provides an easily accessible and reliable water supply. As usual, however, the farm is by no means the oldest settlement on the moor and on both sides of the track lie the tumulus graves of Bronze Age chiefs and the open chambered tombs (cists) that tell of the ancient heritage of farming on Dartmoor. On Chittaford Down above the farmhouse is the route of an ancient moorland trackway whose origins,

Follow the drift lane to the road

like so much on Dartmoor, have long since been lost in history.

6   Beneath England's last castle: Teign Gorge

Introduction

The lands that encircle the moor offer a complete contrast to the bare windswept heather hills. Here, rivers flowing swiftly from the tough granite have trenched deeply into the cracked and contorted rocks that separate moor from plain. Far too steep ever to have been of use to farmers, the valley slopes have remained largely forested and unspoiled. Recent plantations of both coniferous and deciduous trees have added further to the natural grandeur of the valleys.

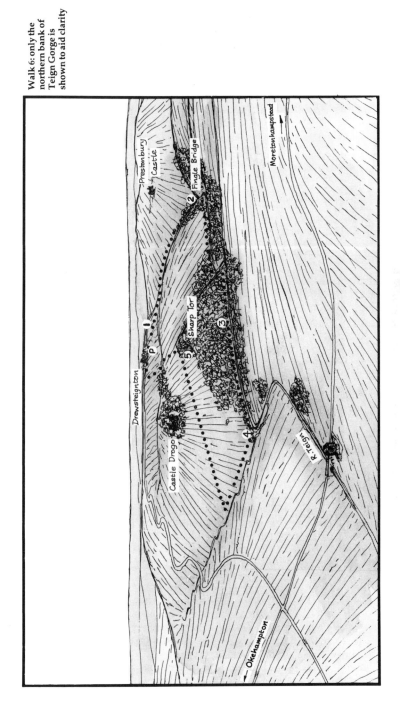

Walk 6: only the northern bank of Teign Gorge is shown to aid clarity

Drewsteignton

Prestonbury Castle

Fingle Bridge

Castle Drogo

Sharp Tor

R. Teign

Okehampton

Moretonhampstead

P

1

2

3

4

5

There are several spectacular moor-edge valleys, but the one best known and visited is the Teign Gorge near Drewsteignton. Here the River Teign has cut a valley 700 ft (213 m) deep along a 5 mile (8 km) course. In 1910 a Mr Drewe, seeking a dramatic site on which to build a granite castle and a place with an implied historical connection with his family, chose the Teign Gorge. Castle Drogo was completed in 1930, and is not only the last English castle but also the last substantial building in England to be constructed from granite.

The walks

🚗 From Okehampton take A30 [Exeter >]. In 8 miles (13 km) turn right [Drewsteignton >]. From Moreton-hampstead A382 [Okehampton >]. In 3 miles (5 km) turn right [Drewsteignton, Castle Drogo >]

(a) Short and easy beside the river. Park at Fingle Bridge. Follow **2,3,4** and return (2 hours).
(b) Longer, to see the gorge from Hunter's Path and Fisherman's Path. Follow **1,2,3,4,5,1** (half a day).

The route

1 Drewsteignton:
WC P ♿ ☕
[Fingle Bridge >]

Drewsteignton (*drew* area held by Drogo; *teign* stream; *ton* settlement) was formerly a very remote hamlet built largely from granite. Many of the buildings date from the 15th century. The hamlet is on a spur of land between two deep valleys on a relatively inaccessible site and just a little too close to the moor to be seen on the main moor-edge road from Okehampton to Exeter. However, isolation and lack of development have preserved Drewsteignton as a symbol of rural charm.

From the village a steep narrow lane leads down the forested slopes of the Teign to Fingle Bridge, a granite structure built in the 17th century probably to replace stepping-stones at a place where two tributary streams tumble into the gorge, cutting steep-sided valleys that provide access across the river.

2 Fingle Bridge. Go up stream opposite restaurant (Fisherman's Path)

Fingle Bridge could never have been of use to more than local traffic, for it is only a backwater in the road pattern of the northern moors. Only foot-paths now trace out the route that once led across the hills to Moretonhampstead. Teign Gorge is much more useful for defence than for communication, and although Castle Drogo was not built for this purpose, its predecessors, Prestonbury Castle and Cranbrook Castle, were constructed with defence very much in mind. These Iron Age earth-works on their hilltop sites overlooking Fingle Bridge are now partly masked by the tree-clad valley flanks, but they still command impressive sites.

(Opposite) **Dappled light filters through the leaves beside the River Teign near Fingle Bridge**

Fisherman's Path follows the River Teign up stream, the forested slopes sweeping down to the river's edge and closing over the water so that only dappled light filters down to the path. Here the river follows a steep course, sometimes tumbling over a bouldery bed and at other places seeming deep and still as it flows in pools. The boulders are a reminder of the power of rivers to erode and transport debris, their rounded shapes an illustration of the way stone can be worn down as it is bounced along by floodwaters. However, only a small part of the scene is the work of the river you see; much more powerful rivers flowed through this gorge towards the end of the Ice Age as deep snows melted from the moors and the meltwater transported the largest boulders. Today these boulders remain where they were dumped 12 000 years ago and the river is forced to twist and turn around them.

The valley sides are covered with flakes of rock that have fallen from the slopes above. Sharp Tor stands prominently as a precipitous cliff, still barren and a continuing source of rock debris. Each winter, rain freezes and expands in the cracks of the exposed rock, prising yet more material loose and

3   sending it tumbling to the gorge below. However, elsewhere the rocks have not been able to resist the forces of the weather as effectively and the slopes have become more gentle. There has been time for a thin soil to develop and for trees to anchor the scree to the slope: the harsh landscape is slowly mellowing.

The steep course of the river is an attraction both to the salmon, which return to spawn each year in the head waters of the Teign above the gorge, and to the men who built the dam over which the

4 Gate. Go up hill [Hunter's Path >]. At beech grove go through gate right (Hunter's Path)

salmon leap. The dam diverts water through a pipe and into a turbine to provide electricity for the castle high above.

Hunter's Path takes us up to the level of the castle and offers a bird's-eye view of the gorge. Following its track above the wooded slopes of the valley and just below the crest of the moors you can clearly see the steep, straight slopes that dive to the water's edge, and the interlocking spurs of land left as the river twists and turns on its journey from the moor. The Hunter's Path is different too, for – in contrast to the shade and still air of the river side – the

5 Sharp Tor [Drewsteignton, Piddledown >]

valley top is in the full light of the sun and there is always a fresh breeze. The bright sunshine and the heather that clings to the thin hillside soil are also an attraction to a wide range of butterflies, from the conspicuous red admiral to blues and browns.

The path opposite the cliff of Sharp Tor leads over Piddledown Common towards Drewsteignton. Just pause for a moment to look at the rock, its twisted and broken pattern created nearly 300 million years ago when it was put under conditions of mighty heat and pressure by the formation of nearby granite. At this time the slate rock was thousands of feet below the surface; now slate and granite have been laid bare, the tougher granite still resisting the forces of the weather more effectively than the slate and forming the higher land on the horizon. Erosion is still continuing and the River Teign continues to cut ever deeper into the Devon countryside, carrying the ancient rocks to the sea and ensuring that the landscape is ever changing.

7 The secret gorge: Lydford

Introduction

Dartmoor is the source of many rivers. Water runs from its rain-washed slopes first into peaty bogs, then into streams, which carve small, shallow valleys. Because these streams flow over the broad undulating surface of the tough granite, the valleys remain insignificant. However, as they leave the moor and cascade down to the encircling lower land, in their rush to the sea over relatively weaker slates they have carved some of the most spectacular gorges in England. One of the most beautiful of these lies at the foot of the western moor next to the hamlet of Lydford. Here, on a path specially constructed by the National Trust, you can wander through the depths of the gorge on an easy path. Later you can see how the gorge has influenced the site and growth of Lydford village, and, lastly, you can visit the moor edge at Widgery Cross to get a bird's-eye view of the Lydford countryside.

◄ From Okehampton take A30, then fork left A386 [Tavistock >]. In 5 miles (8 km), at Dartmoor Inn, turn right [Lydford >] and [Lydford Gorge >]. At end of village 🅿 on right after bridge. Follow the circular clockwise route laid out by the NT

1 Lydford: town guide on Drive 3

The walks

(a) Short and easy to see the gorge. Follow **1,2,3,4, 5,1** (2 hours).

(b) A little longer to include a visit to the village. Follow **1,2,3,4,5,6,7,1** (3 hours).

(c) Longer still to gain the panorama from Widgery Cross. Follow **1 to 8** and return (5 hours).

The route

The gorge. Lydford Gorge is a spectacular defile cut into the slate rocks that surround the moor. The gorge, with its often vertical sides, is set within a much more open valley whose flanks spread out to the plateau. Here, then, you see a valley within a valley. The upper slopes were formed by a river

(Opposite) The
upper path through
the gorge is shaded
by graceful beech
and sycamore

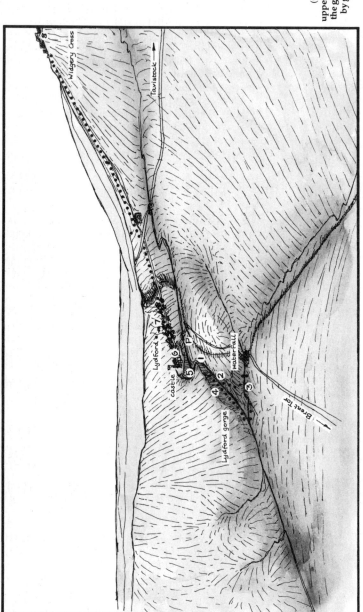

Widgery Cross

→ Tavistock

Lydford

castle

P

waterfall

Lydford gorge

Brent Tor →

8

7

6

5

1

2

4

3

that once flowed out to the River Plym at Tavistock, following a gentle gradient from the moor. The present River Burn is the successor to this river, for the whole of its course is confined to the tough, moor-edge rocks. The waters of the River Lyd, which now tumbles and cascades in the gorge, cut into the floor of its valley when a tributary of the nearby River Tamar eroded back towards the moors and accidentally cut across the line of the River Burn, diverting its headwaters. Lydford Gorge now has a dog-leg plan, a north–south aligned section (from the upper car park to the White Lady waterfall) and a succeeding east–west section below the waterfall. The gorge section has been formed as the headstream of the River Lyd (now diverted from the River Burn) cascades down to join the much lower Lyd valley and the Tamar.

Lydford Gorge illustrates dramatically the way in which the landscape forms. From high up on the forest-clad shoulder of the gorge, you can see down to the sparkling waters of the river far below, across slopes whose thin, often water-soaked soils readily 2 shift and slide under the added burden from the weight of trees. Some trees have secured a firm hold on the rock, sending roots as anchors deep into the cracks, but many species are shallow rooted and are readily carried away. The dominance of thin-stemmed immature trees is evidence of the necessity for continuous renewal to replace those lost by landslides.

Landsliding is most severe on the eastern side of the gorge, where the bands of rock slope down towards the river, acting as natural planes across which slabs of rock and soil can readily move. The path crosses several large slides whose recent occurrence is marked by bare rock above and a chaos of soil and uprooted trees below. Notice how sheets of water wash across the bare rock; it is these sources of water that may have made landsliding more likely, by feeding water into the base of the soil.

3   The dramatic chute of the White Lady waterfall brings water cascading down from the level of the earlier river to that of the new and marks the end of the gorge. Beyond, at the high level, the lower exit and car park of the National Trust lie in the Burn valley, and at the low level the waters of the Lyd flow more gently to the Tamar.

(Opposite) **Water plunges over the spectacular White Lady waterfall from the level of the old river to that of the new**

Each cascade within the gorge marks a band of tough rock that has resisted erosion. At these places, too, the channel narrows and deepens, and 4 there are conspicuous circular pools called pot-holes drilled into the rock by the abrasive action of pebbles sent swirling round and round in eddies.

The upper reaches of the gorge are the most spectacular, for here the Lyd plunges down from the moor, its energy concentrated to such an 5 extent that a truly vertical chasm has been formed. The curved sides of the gorge indicate the location of former pot-holes, the rushing waters of the Lyd cutting the gorge back even closer to the moor edge.

From the NT entrance walk over bridge to the castle

The hamlet and moor. Lydford village has one of the most interesting sites and histories in Devon. It lies at the northern end of Lydford Gorge, where a tributary of the River Lyd joins the river to leave an easily defensible promontory of land. People in the Iron Age were quick to spot this advantage, building a defensive earth bank that is still a conspicuous feature cutting the present village almost in two. Perhaps the same advantages appealed to the Saxons, who founded a town as a defence against the Danes, possibly by reinforcing the Iron Age rampart and capping it with a massive wooden 6 stockade. The Normans, too, maintained Lydford's importance. They built a castle overlooking the gorge (still seen as a mound and ditch behind the church) and then constructed the prominent great square stone keep in the 12th century, expressly to act as a prison – to house offenders against the forest and stannary laws. This was the period when 'Lydford Law' – hang first, judge later – became renowned throughout England.

Today, Lydford is a hamlet on the side of the moor, its trade having been taken away by the better sited towns of Tavistock, Launceston and Okehampton. Even the Castle (formerly White Horse) Inn ceased to be important on the stage-coach route after a road was built across the moor. The main street leads directly towards the moor and its little houses are built mostly of slate and granite. To the left, behind the war memorial and in 7 the angle of the field formed by the lanes, is the oval form of a Bronze Age burial mound, a reminder that this site has been occupied for well over 3000 years.

(Opposite) **Cascades of ferns hang down over the banks of the gorge**

Follow the road to the A386 then go up a narrow track opposite, through the gate and up to the moor

The main Okehampton to Tavistock road that now bypasses Lydford and deprives it of trade also separates the lower and slightly more easily eroded slates of the moor edge from the granites of the moor itself. Above Dartmoor Inn, the land rises towards one of Dartmoor's most accessible tors, Brat Tor, and Widgery Cross. Only rough grazing is possible on these thin, acid soils, and on the flatter slopes near the tor poor drainage has allowed peat to develop on these, the most rainwashed of all Dartmoor's flanks. There is only a jumble of boulders making up the tor, but from its height you can see laid out, as if on a map, the countryside of Cornwall as far as Bodmin Moor. To the south-west the conical hill of Brent Tor seems to lie almost in the shadow of the first outcrop of granite in Cornwall, at Kit Hill. On the lower land below the moor a patchwork of fields covers the plateau top, cut in places by the dark green gashes of deep, wooded valleys. The nearest of these is Lydford Gorge, its dog-leg plan quite easy to see, and below, on the moorland slopes to the right of Widgery Cross and cutting round behind it, lies the source of the River Lyd – a stream whose insignificant waters here look quite incapable of cutting a spectacular gorge just 2 miles further on.

8 Tumbling waters: Becky Falls, Manaton

Introduction

The northern edge of Dartmoor is fretted by deeply trenched rivers, whose waters tumble from the moorland heights to the surrounding lowland within a mile or two. The trenched valley of the River Bovey not only provides a pleasant walk along a shaded riverside, but also offers the drama of a boulder-strewn waterfall and wide vistas from the nearby tors.

This is an especially difficult landscape for the traveller, its steep slopes and narrow valleys providing little opportunity for road building. No roads follow the valley bottom or the moorland top; instead they use the shoulder of the moors, only dipping on to the valley to cross it before climbing swiftly out again. Similarly, there is little room for building, and even hamlets have a strung-out form. In consequence, this area remains relatively peaceful and quiet, its hamlets little disturbed by recent building.

From Bovey Tracey take B3344 [Manaton >]. On hill fork left [Hay Tor >]. Beyond Hay Tor turn right [Hound Tor >]. P

The walks

(a) Short and easy to see Becky Falls and the hamlet of Manaton. Follow **4,3** (2 hours).

(b) To include the view from Hound Tor. Follow **1,2,3,4,1** (allow half a day).

Walks 108

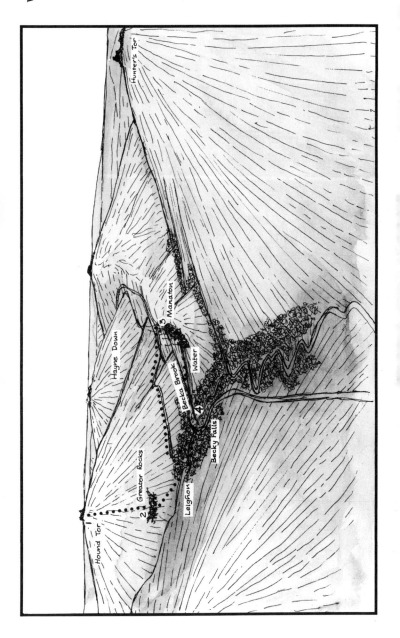

Hunter's Tor

Hayne Down

Manaton

Becka Brook

Water

Becky Falls

Greator Rocks

Leighon

Hound Tor

5

4

2

The route

1 Houndtor rocks

Hound Tor forms the head of a wide valley which carries part of the waters that eventually tumble over the rocks at Becky Falls. Distant Hunter's Tor caps the far side of the Bovey valley into which Becka Brook finally flows. Both Hound Tor and Hunter's Tor have evidence of ancient settlements. The latter is capped by an Iron Age Fort and in the shadow of Hound Tor lies evidence not only of a medieval hamlet but also of ancient Bronze Age

2 Medieval village

people (marked 'cist' on maps). However, when these people looked across the Becka and Bovey valleys, they would not have seen the open moorland and deep, wooded valley we see today. Rather they would have seen a landscape completely clothed in woodland, thick with oak and elm in the valleys and with somewhat thinner stands of oak and birch on the moorland shoulders. Probably only the highest tors were forest free. Since that time, over 2000 years ago, pressure to use any but the steepest land for farming has led to the removal of virtually all the upland forest, and the continued grazing by sheep ensures that no sapling will survive.

People have tried to use the upland moor intensively many times. Probably during the Bronze Age the climate was still good enough to allow them to do so, but by medieval times conditions were much worse. Below Hound Tor, in the dip before Greator Rocks and near to a natural spring that emerges from the granite, lie the remains of about eight houses, three barns and a longhouse surrounded by stone-built field walls. Remains of kilns formerly used to dry corn have been discovered, indicating that the people cultivated the land. It must have been a hard struggle, finally lost when the Black Death reached Dartmoor in the middle of the 14th century.

From Great Tor walk down hill, cross footbridge and follow track to Leighon Farm, then by road follow the shoulder of the hill to Manaton

The valley of the Becka Brook between Leighon and Manaton is wide and has gentle sides and its lower elevation makes it more successful farming country than the upper moors. As a result, extensive rough grazing is replaced by a patchwork of cultivated and pasture fields, and the range of farming activities has been widened to include cattle. However, even in the shelter of the valley, the good land is not sufficiently extensive to provide a living for more than a small number of

(Opposite) **Water tumbling between the giant blocks of granite that make the Becky Falls**

people, and Manaton, the largest settlement in the valley, has not grown beyond the size of a hamlet.

3 Steep slopes nearby and narrow, hedge-lined roads continue to restrict accessibility and prevent the charm being spoilt by housing development. In Victorian times a railway was built through the Bovey valley and a station constructed at nearby Lustleigh. At this time Manaton was busier than it is today and, since the closure and dismantling of the railway in 1930, like other parts of the country, the Bovey valley has become less accessible.

The sprawling form of Manaton hamlet may be a result of the foundation of several separate settlements along the road. Today the church is well over half a mile away from the shops, which are now clustered at the eastern end, called Water.

Follow the road. [Becky Falls >] opposite 🅿

4 Becky Falls
The gentle slopes of the upper Becka valley end abruptly at Becky Falls. Here the tough granite ends and weaker slates begin, a change clearly etched out by the stream such that the falls mark the step down from granite to slate. The falls are notable not only for their pleasant shaded aspect but also for the huge granite boulders that choke the river bed. These falls are best seen after a period of heavy rain, when they rush and tumble over the boulders sending sparkling mists into the air. However, in quieter mood, and during dry weather, the boulders trap the water, sending it scudding around them. Yet in no way can this pleasant stream move the boulders that litter its bed. These, like so many of the Dartmoor boulders, were moved by much more powerful waters carrying melting snow from the moors at the end of the last Ice Age.

From opposite falls follow the minor road to Leighon and return to Hound Tor

9 Moorland's hidden village: Widecombe and Hound Tor

Introduction
Although people have braved the elements on Dartmoor for thousands of years, by the time the Saxons advanced westwards to Devon, the climate was mostly too severe to allow settlement anywhere but in a sheltered valley. However, the tough granite has not yielded to the streams flowing over it and deep valleys are rare. Thus, where the Webburn river has cut into an area of weaker rock and left an enclave surrounded by high downs, it was a natural place for a settlement.

The flat, marshy floor of the Webburn river must have been very obvious to the Saxon colonisers because they named their hamlet

(Opposite) **The quiet village green at Manaton**

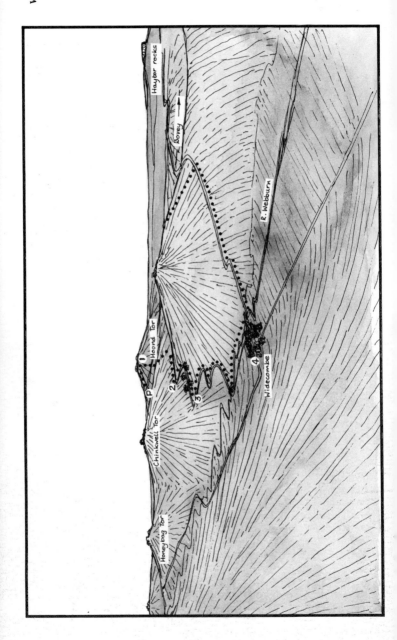

Honeybag Tor

Chinkwell Tor

Hound Tor

Haytor rocks

Bovey

R. Webburn

Widecombe

P

1

2

3

4

Widecombe (willow valley) after the willow trees that flourished on the damp flood plain. The site of Widecombe is still best observed on foot by approaching it over the moors, in this case from nearby Hound Tor.

From Bovey Tracey take B3344 [Manaton >]. On hill fork left [Hay Tor >]. Beyond Hay Tor turn right [Hound Tor >]. 🅿

The walks

(a) Short and easy to walk down into Widecombe and back again. Follow **2,3,4,2** (1½ hours).

(b) Longer, to include the views from Hound Tor. Follow **1,2,3,4,1** (half a day).

The route

Walk to Hound Tor

1 Hound Tor lies just a few hundred yards from the car park, up a grassy slope through which project the clitter stones once prised from the tor rocks by frost and sent bouncing down hill. The tor has a central avenue, a line of weakness from which all the stone has gone. Now stripped of soil and exposed to the weather, the remaining tor stones rest one upon another, their interlocking form like a giant Legoland toy. Notice how the blocks have been rounded at the edges by the weather. Indeed some of the stones have been eroded back so far that they can be rocked to and fro.

The massive granite blocks of Hound Tor with Hamel Down beyond

As you approach Hound Tor, the granite stones look like the dark and foreboding ramparts of a medieval castle, and in this case the 'drawbridge' that gives easy access to the top is on the far side. Whether from the top or bottom of the rocks, there is a broad view north across the wooded valley of the River Bovey, which has cut deeply into the softer rocks that surround the moors. To the south stands the bold mass of Hay Tor (View 1), its quarries clearly seen, looking like bites taken out of the lower slopes.

Everywhere on these moors are the signs of past civilisation: the oval burial mounds of Bronze Age chieftains (tumuli); the hut circles of the same age; the standing stones (menhirs), which may have religious significance and are of uncertain age. Perhaps most remarkable of all is the medieval hamlet whose remains lie half-buried in the bracken on the northern slopes of Hound Tor. The remains of several communal longhouses, inter-connecting paths and walled paddocks date from the 13th century (see Walk 8). Here people lived alongside their animals as they sheltered from the cold winters, people at one end of the house and animals at the other.

Walk along the road then turn right beside the stream, walking in a saddle between tors until the Widecombe road is reached

The lower ground between the moors is made from granite that has weathered less well and in consequence was stripped away more rapidly during the Ice Age. Where partly disintegrated blocks of granite remain in situ, such as on most moors, the rock allows water to pass through it relatively easily and the surface remains dry. On the other hand, where it has been stripped away more thoroughly – and especially in saddle-shaped depressions along the moors – water cannot seep

2 away at all readily and it commonly forms bogs. Over many years such bogs preserve the remains of plants that grow on them, finally producing peat. Peat cutting has, for centuries, been a widespread moorland activity, the peat being stacked to dry and then used for fuel. The route over to the Widecombe road runs across such a boggy depression.

3 The little hamlet of Bone Hill straggles down the valley slope leading from the tors to Widecombe. This is the highest possible level of settlement built at the very limit of cultivation. Everywhere around lie granite boulders showing how close is the rock to the surface in these fields. The field walls, too,

(Opposite) **Granite-built Widecombe church, the 'Cathedral of the Moors'**

are made of huge boulders, rolled from the fields in an attempt to clear the land. Each group of houses is located on a tiny flat bench on a generally steep slope.

4 Widecombe
P wc 🐾 ♨ 📶 ⊘ M

The valley bottom is not inhabited, for even in this age of better drainage techniques, the land is still marshy. In fact Widecombe is not actually on the valley bottom at all, but on a knoll of granite rising from it, the first house in the village being at the foot of the knoll, and the church and oldest houses at the top. The village is built around a green, still marked by a line of granite boulders. Not all the gravestones in the nearby churchyard are made of granite, however, for it must have been difficult (and expensive) work hewing such tough stone.

[Bovey Tracey >] to valley top then take grassy track left parallel to road and return to Hound Tor

The return along the Haytor road again rises steeply, with outcrops of granite, so-called side-tors, on both sides. In these rocks some of the opaque pink and white crystals of feldspar are several inches long. You can see them best by turning over a piece of granite that has been face down in the soil, for any exposed face is sure to be covered with pale grey–green lichen, which clings to the rock and contributes to its decay. However, as the tors show, rocks decay quietly and unobtrusively.

10   The devil's way: Grimspound

Introduction
Wherever you walk on Dartmoor, you will find the remains of ancient settlements of the Bronze Age. These are traces of life on the moor when the climate was both warmer and drier. Most common are the oval early burial mounds (tumuli) of Bronze Age chieftains. There are still several hundred on the moor, along with piles of stones (cairns) on ridge tops. These features take on a variety of forms. Some, called cists, can be seen to have coffin structures in their centres, where earth from the tumulus has been removed and the coffins, made from large slabs of granite, left open; others have a ring of standing-stones around them.

It is the standing-stones that most catch the imagination, some-times arranged in enigmatic circles as though for some form of religious worship, at other times arranged in rows as though marking out ancient tracks. However, most inspiring of all are the circular enclosing walls (pounds) built by Bronze Age people as a form of village-cum-corral. Grimspound ('the devil's enclosure') is the most striking, lying high on the moor above Widecombe and containing the remains of 24 circular huts.

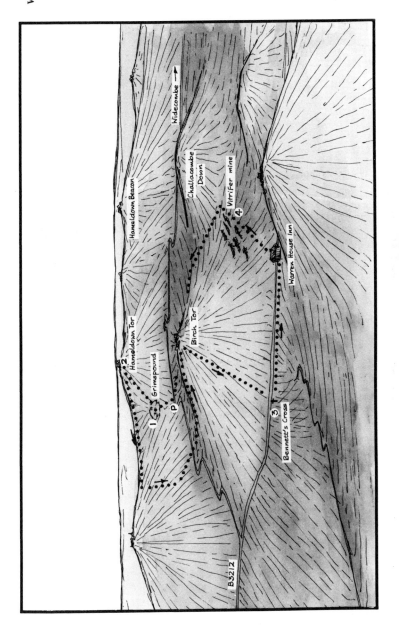

Hameldown Beacon

Widecombe →

Challacombe
Down

Hameldown Tor

Vitrifer mine

4

Grimspound

2

P

Birch Tor

Warren House Inn

1

3

Bennett's Cross

B3212

◄ From
Moretonhampstead
take B3212
[Yelverton >].
At Challacombe
Cross, left
[Widecombe >].
In 1½ miles (2.4 km)
🅿, broad track to
Grimspound

The walks

(a) Short and easy from the car park at Grims-pound to see the hut circles and gain a view from Hameldown Tor above. Follow **1,2** and return (1 hour).

(b) Longer, to include a walk to the old tin mines of Vitrifer and Birch Tor and pass stone rows and hut circles. Follow **1,2,3,4** (half a day).

The route

1 Grimspound

Although the climate was milder when Bronze Age people lived at Grimspound, their lives were governed by their environment, for the enclosure lies in the shelter of a fold in the slopes leading from Hamel Down, beside a stream providing a reliable water supply. At this time the main valley floor would have been forested and marshy; the settlement is on the more lightly wooded slopes, which were easier to clear.

Walk up slope to Hameldown Tor

2

It is difficult to imagine Hamel Down cloaked in birch, ash, oak and elm, but we must remember to view Grimspound as its builders saw it, as a clearing in the woodland. Generation after generation of clearance, of using trees for timber and firewood and in a multitude of other ways, stripped the woodland and left pasture on which animals could graze. However, during this period the climate became progressively more severe, the rainfall greater and the soils more leached by the water that washed through them. Eventually, there were insufficient nutrients for grass to grow, and heather became dominant, for its low nutrient needs were a sure recipe for success. This is how we see it today: open, treeless, with poor soils and heather cover, an apparently inhospitable place in which to site a village – unless you remember how the Bronze Age people saw it. From Hamel Down, Bronze Age people would not have seen mile after mile of heather moor and a skyline capped with tors; instead they would have seen forested valleys and wooded hills. Today from Hamel Down you can see westwards towards the heart of the moor and eastwards to the low ground of the moor edge, where the slopes of the steep-sided valleys still remain forested. Beyond the first bridge of Easdon Tor lies the trench of the River Bovey, still within the granite, then beyond this the broad back of Mardon Down, whose slopes lead off the moor and are deeply scored by the valley of the Teign.

(Opposite) **The impressive circular boundary wall at Grimspound is now cut by the trail made by holiday-makers keen for a view from the hill top**

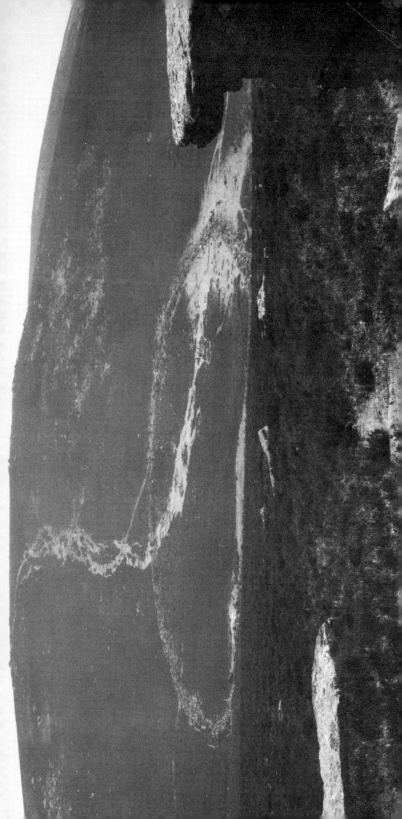

From Hamel Down you can see the grand scale of the landscape and the more intimate scale produced by millennia of cultivation. Below lies Grimspound, built during the first period of moorland cultivation. To the left and a little further down the valley, beside Challacombe Farm and on the flanks of Challacombe Down, are the terraced fields enclosed by stone walls belonging to a period of cultivation 2000 years later, an attempt by people in the Middle Ages to extend cultivation to 1300 ft (396 m) above sea level; however, in a climate far worse than in the Bronze Age they were doomed to failure. Today Challacombe Farm represents the more enduring face of pastoral farming.

The view from Hamel Down leads over the valley to another part of man's attempt to gain a living from the moors. Here, between Challacombe Down and Birch Tor, lies the scored landscape of the Vitrifer tin mines. Late into the 19th century this valley was not as quiet as you see it today, but full of the noise from the miners, their engines and their machinery.

Walk north to saddle, then left across Birch Tor to main road at Bennett's Cross

3

The route over the broad back of Birch Tor leads on to the old road across the moors, its course still marked by crude stone medieval crosses such as Bennett's Cross. Nearby Warren House Inn appears to be just another wayside coaching stop along this highway. However, a hundred years ago it was surrounded by the shacks and tents of a miners' camp, for it was a focal point for those working deep underground in the tin mines.

Take footpath opposite Warren House Inn into valley between Birch Tor and Challacombe Down to Vitrifer tin mines

4

Take care on the walk through the mines, for there are many deep clefts remaining from the time of the mining boom. To walk over it you would think the miners dug at random, hoping to make a lucky strike, yet their exploration of the ground was undertaken with care and precision. All the workings have an east–west alignment, similar to those at Kit Hill (View 3) and elsewhere, for the miners knew the lie of the geological formation in which the lodes were located. As you leave the mine and look across to Grimspound, you may care to reflect on the changing history of this valley.

Keep left of farm to regain the road at Grimspound

11 Deep among the hills: Dartmeet

Introduction
The River Dart is the major river of the moors. Its headwaters, which begin high among the northern tors, first flow south and east in wide, open valleys, through extensive stretches of blanketing bog. However, the Dart is unusual because there is no headwater stream to

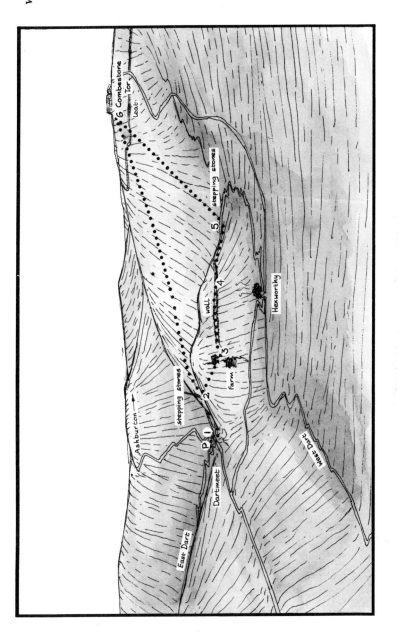

East Dart

Ashburton →

Dartmeet

P 1

stepping stones

2

farm 3

wall

4

West Dart

Hexworthy

5 stepping stones

Leat

6 Combestone Tor

which the others are tributaries; instead, two branches of equal size drain across the moor, converging on to one trunk stream only as they near the upland edge. Dartmeet, where the East and West Dart meet at right angles, marks not just a convergence of water but also a change of river scene, for down stream the united river begins to trench deeply into the granite as it makes a swift descent to the surrounding plain. Above Dartmeet lie high, heather-covered, stone-capped hills and peat-filled valleys; below there is a landscape of steep slopes and forests. This change of scene is most easily observed on the walk from Dartmeet Bridge to Combestone Tor, one of the most easterly tors of the moor.

The walks

(a) Short and easy to see the meander bend of the West Dart river. Follow **1,2,3,4,5** and return (1½ hours).

(b) Longer, to walk halfway up the down to the downside stones of Combestone Tor and across the stepping-stones. Follow **1,2,3,4,5,6,1** (3 hours).

The route

From Ashburton take B3357 [Princetown >]. P at Dartmeet. Dartmeet P ☂ WC

Dartmeet is a tiny hamlet situated at one corner of the ancient Royal Forest of Dartmoor. To the north and west of the confluence, game could be hunted only by permission of the King. Even in Norman times the land was not wooded, but had long been cleared for farming. The steep slopes nearby probably contain as much wood today as has been present for a thousand years.

1 Clapper bridge beside **P**. Cross road bridge and walk up hill. Follow [footpath >] on left next to garage, turning down to river to see stepping-stones

Dartmeet is also on an ancient track across the moors connecting the monastic foundations of Buckfast and Tavistock. Although there was sufficient passing traffic to warrant the building of a clapper bridge of rough granite slabs, the infertile moorland could never support many people and no substantial settlement grew. The clapper bridge spans the East Dart, but the West Dart can still only be crossed by stepping-stones made from large granite boulders. In summer these boulders are usually uncovered and easy to cross. (They will be needed for the return from Combestone Tor.) However, pleasant though the Dart may be in dry weather, rain on the moors soon turns the river into a torrent of considerable power and water frequently washes over the stepping-stones, even in summer.

Granite is often believed to be not only tough but also watertight. The fenced spring in the field

(Opposite) **The granite stepping-stones that cross the West Dart river**

above the stepping-stones gives the lie to this belief, for here water constantly gushes, fed by nothing more than rainwater seepage through the soil and between blocks of rotting granite.

2 Walk up hill past fenced spring and into lane

Blocks of granite must have lain everywhere over these hill slopes, much as they do in the areas near the tors today. It is a tribute to the patience of generations of farmers that so few fields now contain boulders; instead they have been put to use making dry-stone walls. Here, field boundaries are very much a matter of convenience: if a field boulder is too large to move, better by far to build the field wall to incorporate it. The strange orientation of many of the nearby walls may well be explained by this pragmatic approach. Indeed the field sizes may even be a product of the same need to dispose of unwanted boulders: the more boulders, the more wall, the smaller the field!

3 Follow lane over brow of hill and down to farmyard, then across yard and follow [footpath >]. (Note: If Dartmeet stepping-stones are impassable, walk to Combestone by the road through Hexworthy and return the same way)

The track beyond the farm leads out on to a promontory of land encircled by a great bend of the West Dart. Up stream the landscape opens out to give views to the high central moors, dissected by only a shallow river valley. By contrast, as the river flows round the Hexworthy bend it begins to cut more deeply into the rock where its bed follows a steeper course. From this vantage point it is easy to see how a river works. On each curve the inside of the bend shows buff-coloured gravel bands deposited by the river in a place of slack gradient; in contrast, on the outside bend water sweeps against the bank, undercutting the soil and causing the bank to collapse. The vantage point itself has been created by thousands of years of river action cutting away at the foot of the slope.

4

5 Cross stepping-stones and walk up hill to the valley-side pile of rocks of Combestone Tor

The stepping-stones (called Week Ford) provide an opportunity to see the action of the water close at hand. The coarse sandy material of the bank is unstable and makes the bank collapse. This is growan, the remains of granite that has been eroded by rain water high on the moor and carried in fragments by the river. The stepping-stones show still unweathered granite, clearly composed of interlocking crystals. Growan is made mostly of the grey quartz, all that remains after the pink and white feldspar crystals have been rotted away by the acid water of the peat bogs. Notice how the stepping-stones are placed where the river's course is straight. Here the banks are not undercut, as they would be on a curving stretch of the river, and the bed is uniformly shallow: man has thus been able to take advantage of the work of Nature.

The walk to Combestone Tor allows you to gain a perspective of the sweep of the river and to look down stream to the ever deepening and forest-clad valley of the 'united' Dart. Today it looks as though it has been peaceful farmland for a thousand years, yet both the rough ground near the stepping-stones and the dry channel that cuts along the contour below the tor are man-made. Wheal Emma Leat is a now abandoned channel for carrying water to a number of copper mines. There are many spoil heaps nearby, some just east of the track beside the

6 Combestone Tor road and others (Henroot Wheals and Hooten mines) are a little up hill of the tor. These are reminders of the days when this area, as so many others on Dartmoor, resounded to the noise of crushing hammers.

Walk directly down hill along the track past Combestone Farm to stepping-stones over the West Dart

From the tor you can see some faint parallel ridges on the hill slope opposite. These 'reaves', best seen when illuminated by a low-angled evening sun, are 4000-year-old field boundaries, a reminder of the long history of man's attempt to tame Dartmoor's wilderness.

12   By the sparkling stream: New Bridge

Introduction

The River Dart leaves the high moors in spectacular style. Within 6 miles (10 km) it falls nearly 600 ft (180 m), cutting a spectacular wooded gorge whose great curves offer some of the most delightful scenery in South Devon. Unlike most river valleys, which are quickly used for communication through upland areas, the Dart's steeply trenched valley is more of a hindrance than a help. There is no flat floodplain on which to build a road, and following its winding course almost doubles the length of journey from plain to moor. Because of these difficulties, the moorland road from Ashburton to Dartmeet avoids the valley as much as possible, only diving down the steep sides to cross the river, then climbing straight out again. With so little contact between road and river, the motorist gets little opportunity to sample the delights of this part of the Dart valley. But at New Bridge a stretch of common land on one bank and National Trust property on the other offer short walks by the tumbling waters of Dartmoor's most famous river.

The walk

New Bridge lies midway between Ashburton and Dartmeet on B3357

The walk across common land downstream from the car park is short and easy (1½ hours). It can be extended by walking through the woodland (Cleave Wood) on the bank opposite the car park (total 2½ hours).

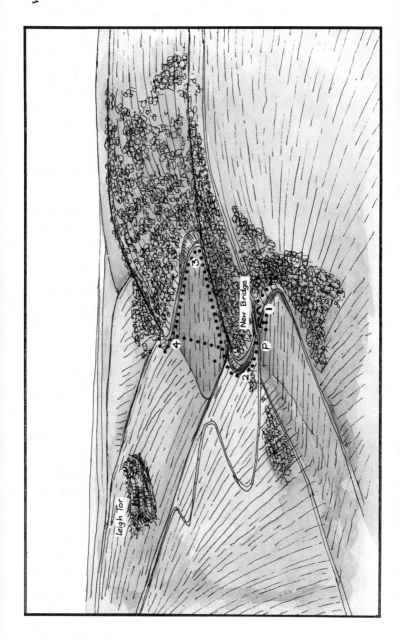

The route

The builders of the 15th century New Bridge needed to find not only a relatively gentle slope leading from both banks, but also an outcrop of rock in the middle of the river to provide the base for a pier, because the river was too wide to be spanned easily by a single arch. Both up stream and down stream the curving river throws water hard against its banks, creating deep pools and precipitous slopes. The site they chose is therefore on one of the few straight river reaches, where the water flows evenly and the river is uniformly shallow. Even here, however, the river bed has trenched quite deeply below its banks and this has required the bridge to be built high.

Although New Bridge is on the edge of Dartmoor, the river flows over grey slates rather than moorland granite. The slates rise steeply to the surface to give a series of 'steps' or 'ledges' over which the river cascades.

The high cliff, just down stream of the bridge, has been cut by the river as it sweeps first to the left, throwing the force of its water against the near bank, then, as it veers away and sweeps to the right, a cliff is cut on the far bank allowing the footpath to return to the level floodplain.

The flat pastureland beside the river (Spitchwick Common) shows the extent to which the water has cut across the floor of the gorge. All this land has been carved out of the solid rock, and boulders used by the river to wear away the banks still lie half exposed in the turf.

Follow the curve of the river and look closely at the river-cut cliff; below it lies the deep pool and the main thread of fast-flowing water, which is still actively scouring away at the rock leaving an overhanging ledge just above river level. By contrast, fine material has settled on the near bank, showing where the current is much reduced. Down stream the river straightens again, the undercutting ceases and the cliff merges into a slope sufficiently gentle to allow soil to form and oak and birch woods to thrive.

At first you may think the bouldery bed of the river hints at the contrast between summer and winter flows. In summer the water is clear, its speed hardly sufficient to move a grain of sand. However, even the power of water that must develop in a winter storm is now insufficient to rip the boulders from the bed and tumble them further down towards the sea. These granite boulders

1 New Bridge
🅿 WC ♿

Walk under bridge
and follow footpath
down stream

2 River cliff

3

travelled several miles from the moors long ago when, at the end of the Ice Age, the river was far more powerful than it is today.

4 View to Leigh Tor on left

High on the left is the prominent crag of Leigh Tor, its straight line marking the location of a band of tough rock that has resisted all attempts by the forces of the weather to subdue it. Although most Dartmoor tors are granite, this is not the only rock from which tors are made: Leigh Tor is cut in slates, its alignment paralleling that of the bands of rock forming the bed of the river. In fact this tough rock is the cause of the narrowing valley that lies ahead.

At the road turn right and follow it down stream until the road diverges from the river. Then return to New Bridge

The last part of the walk, beside the road, offers pretty views of the tree-lined river in its gorge. The river can hardly be contained in its channel here and the exposed roots of trees show where the winter floodwaters regularly tear at the banks. This fast-flowing water is ideal for trout. Look for the sleek brown forms of the fish flicking their tails as they lie motionless, head-on to the current in the pools between the cascades. Watching the trout provides an excuse for dawdling in this beautiful valley before returning to New Bridge.

13 Devon's guardian: Berry Head

Introduction

Berry Head stands out to sea as the southernmost of the rocky headland 'jaws' that enclose and protect Tor Bay. When storm winds blow up the English Channel from the south-west, Berry Head takes the brunt of the pounding, allowing ships to ride safely at anchor in the bay. Brixham, once one of the world's most famous fishing ports, shelters directly in the lee of this limestone bastion, its long concrete and stone breakwater thrust out for a kilometre into the bay to provide extra protection from the infrequent northeasterlies.

Berry Head has offered more than just physical protection from the storm-tossed waves. To the ancient Iron Age people it provided a safe place for retreat in times of attack; to Drake's kinsfolk it was a viewpoint to the approaching Armada; to the British, threatened by Napoleonic invasion and by the Germans during the Second World War, it has provided an early warning station and an easily defended gun emplacement. Today it still performs vital town functions of lighthouse and coastguard lookout. It also provides a commanding vantage point for the visitor.

Berry Head is a fascinating demonstration of the way people have used a natural feature to their advantage over thousands of years. Many of the remains are easy both to see and to visit: you can even sit and have a cup of tea surrounded by the sheltering walls of the 18th century fort.

(Opposite) **Ledges of rock cut across the path of the River Dart at New Bridge**

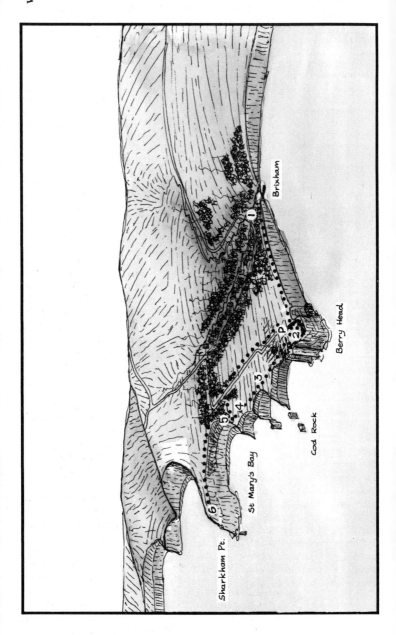

Brixham

Berry Head

Cod Rock

St Mary's Bay

Sharkham Pt.

The walks

⇘ Take A3022
Torbay ring road
south to Brixham.
From Brixham centre
B3205 [Kingswear >]
for ½ mile (1 km);
turn left [swimming
pool, Berry
Head >]. At junction
fork right and
continue to **P** at end

(a) The cliff-top walk on level ground is short and
easy. Follow **2,3,4,5,2** (1½ hours), or, to see
Sharkham Point, **2,3,4,5,6,2** (2½ hours).
(b) The walk from Brixham adds a pleasant visit to
an interesting port and tourist resort and takes
nearly half a day. Follow **1,2,3,4,5,6,2,1**.

The route

Follow the coastal
footpath from the
coastguard station
near the breakwater
[Berry Head >]

2 Berry Head fort

The fort, which was enlarged and strengthened as
a defence against Napoleon, still dominates the
head. From its massive ramparts there is a sweeping view across Torbay to the opposing 'jaw',
which ends in the rocks of Hope's Nose (View 2).
Both headlands stand proud because they are made
of tough, massive rocks. Berry Head is made from a
dove-grey limestone, in contrast to the weaker red
sandstones that have been worn back into the
sweeping arc of the bay. The headland has been
extensively quarried for building stone, the vast
pit on the northern side looking like a great bite
gnawed from its great flank. Yet strangely the rock,
which still withstands the waves so staunchly, has
a top planed as flat as a board. Inland the constant
height is maintained for over a mile (2 km) before
being backed by higher, rolling hills. This flat
surface was formed millions of years ago when the
headland lay at sea level and was trimmed by the
waves right back to the distant hills, which now
form an old shoreline. At that time the headland
probably lay covered by a sandy beach, although all
trace of the sand has long since been washed away.

3 You can see the processes of wave action still
operating today as they pound relentlessly against
the foot of the cliffs. The rocky islets (Mew Stone
and Cod Rock) show former positions of the headland, and Durl Rock, a little further along, will also
soon be completely severed from the cliff. Berry
Head may look everlasting, but it is getting smaller
as the years pass.

4   The cliffs beyond Durl Head reveal the ancient
rocks clearly. From above a cave excavated by wave
attack you can look back to Durl Head and see the
layers of rock rise out of the sea in a massive curve.
These rocks were once formed as level sheets below
the sea, their present arched and cracked layers
providing a hint of the time, 300 million years ago,
when both Berry Head and Durl Head were part of
a range of mountains. The cracks that were formed
as the rock was bent upwards now form the
Achilles' heel of the cliff, providing the opportunity

Berry Head 133

for waves to demolish the cliff block by block. But the wave action serves another purpose. By leaving ledges where blocks have been prised away, the cliffs offer excellent nesting sites for fulmars, razorbills, gulls and many other birds.

Footpath returns to Brixham (or continue into bay)

St Mary's Bay is made of much weaker stuff than the headland, as is strikingly revealed in its crumbling and falling cliffs. Here, beds of slates and shales cracked into thin plates, rather than the massive blocks of limestone, not only fall ready prey to wave attack, but are also prone to landslides and collapse. The future of holiday homes and cafés in this exposed bay is far less secure than in sheltered Brixham. Only the resistant limestone of distant Sharkham Point is preventing a disastrous rate of cliff erosion.

5

6 Sharkham Point

Sharkham Point is very similar to Berry Head, but it offers a chance to look along the southern coast. Its succession of bays are picked out in weak rocks by wave attack and the intervening headlands of tougher rock still stand proud. Yet all these minor headlands pale beside the massive bulk of Berry Head, which, in its resistance to wave attack, really seems like Devon's guardian.

RAZOR-STROP FUNGUS

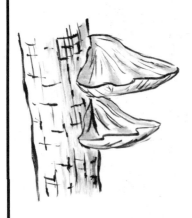

With its distinctive brown surface and creamy white underbelly, this dinner-plate sized fungus is commonly found projecting from trunks of the silver birch. Rupturing the bark and feeding on the nutrients contained within the trunk, the razor-strop slowly swells for several years before releasing thousands of spores from pores on its lower surface. It is one of a wide range of bracket fungi, which include the red–brown Beefsteak Fungus that 'bleeds' when cut.

(Opposite) **Contorted bands of rock seen curving outwards in the cliffs of Berry Head where the cliff-top has been planed flat by an ancient sea**

A classic journey by rail from Paignton to Kingswear

Introduction

The South Devon area has never been an easy place for any form of communication. Valleys cut deep trenches in the coastal plateau, and great arms of the sea reach far into the land. The estuaries in particular have forced road and railway lines to choose routes a long way from the coast, leaving the regions near the sea severely isolated. When the railway was built along the coast westwards from Dawlish in 1846, it was forced inland to Newton Abbot because of the Teign estuary. From here the line cut across the South Hams peninsula, heading for

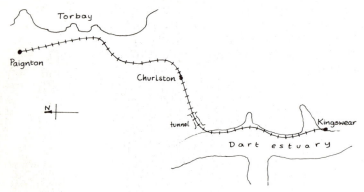

Classic rail route

Plymouth via Totnes. To connect the main line with the coast and its seaside towns, whose sandy beaches offered the prospect of much tourist traffic, spurs were run southwards, one to the little port of Kingsbridge (1893), the other (1848–64) from Newton Abbot by way of Torbay, to end at Kingswear opposite Dartmouth. In 1872 a spur was built from Totnes northwards along the Dart valley to connect with Buckfast.

These spur lines could only be viable provided there was no other competition and with the arrival of motor transport all the spur lines, other than that connecting Newton Abbot to Torbay, became progressively underused and were finally closed. The Dart valley spur and the Paignton to Kingswear spur were later acquired by railway enthusiasts, who now operate regular services. The route described here concentrates on the Paignton to Kingswear section of the system.

(Opposite) **A steam train leaves Kingsbridge heading for the upper ferry halt, along a track which runs on an embankment in the estuary because the valley slopes are so steep**

The journey

This is a short section of railway taking about half an hour each way. Walks 3a and 3b along the Dart estuary are recommended.

The route

The route was initially intended to run from Paignton behind the promenade, across the narrow neck of land between Paignton and Brixham, crossing the River Dart and entering Dartmouth from the north. However, powerful local objection to the last part of the route forced the railway builders to abandon the Dart crossing. Instead they had to content themselves with a terminus at Kingswear on the bank opposite Dartmouth, a location that not only prevented the growth of trade in Dartmouth, but also robbed the railway of considerable potential revenue and contributed to its eventual closure.

1   At Paignton the railway is set amid the bustle of the town a stone's throw from the beach. Just to the south of the town a deep cutting into the rich red sandstone Torbay rocks leads the route below roads and houses to emerge on the edge of Goodrington Sands. The point of this diversion to the sea is to make use of a narrow coastal bench that lies on the cliff-top at Goodrington and avoids the need for a deep cutting through Sugar Loaf Hill on which the village stands.

2   The coastside section of 2 km provides ample time to look across Torbay and see the flat top of Berry Head (Walk 13) jutting out to sea beyond the fishing port of Brixham. Below, prominent rocky shore alternates with re-entrant sandy beach as successive bands of tough red sandstone and weak red shale rock are crossed.

The railway was a relatively early arrival on the rural scene, and its viaduct and embankment had been in place for over half a century when Goodrington began to expand towards the sea. Today, rows of houses and bungalows stretch down towards the sea, their views obstructed by the 'iron road'.

Beyond Goodrington the track has been built in sweeping curves designed to gain height in preparation for cresting the divide that separates
3   Torbay from the Dart valley. Embankments change to cuttings as the crest station of Churlston is reached. At Churlston the track is at a height of over 196 ft (60 m), yet within 2 miles (3 km) it is

down to sea level, a swift change in height that needed substantial engineering skill.

The neck of land between Torbay and the Dart is narrow because it is formed in deep red shale rocks whose weak structure has led to their rapid erosion. The shales weather to yield rich clay soils: potentially good for farming, but poor to drain. As a result, many surface streams have formed, carving steep-sided valleys as they rush towards the river.

In an attempt to avoid the steep valley sides, the railway engineers preferred to follow a narrow ridge of higher land, leaving valleys to both left and right. This did not, however, solve the problem of losing height, and despite driving the Greenway tunnel through a high spur of land, on leaving the tunnel the track is still nearly 200 ft (60 m) above sea level and facing a wooded hill slope that plunges directly down to the sea. The solution has been to cut a long inclined path diagonally across 4 the lower slopes, finally to emerge beside the Dart estuary. From here the track is mostly laid on an artificial embankment which, together with more embankment to bridge two shallow inlets, enables trains to reach Kingswear station beside the Dartmouth ferry. From the station you can wander through the quiet streets of Kingswear or pause beside the ferry and look towards Dartmouth, the Walk 3 original destination of the railway.

SYCAMORE

(90 ft; 30 m)

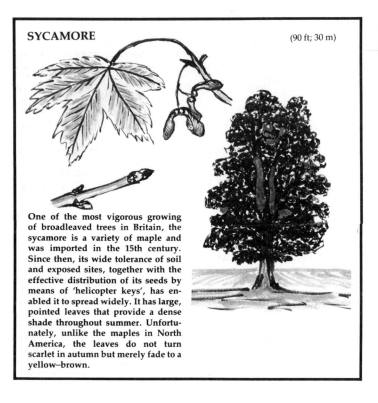

One of the most vigorous growing of broadleaved trees in Britain, the sycamore is a variety of maple and was imported in the 15th century. Since then, its wide tolerance of soil and exposed sites, together with the effective distribution of its seeds by means of 'helicopter keys', has enabled it to spread widely. It has large, pointed leaves that provide a dense shade throughout summer. Unfortunately, unlike the maples in North America, the leaves do not turn scarlet in autumn but merely fade to a yellow–brown.

Appendix: other useful information

Within reach of Torbay

Brixham: nautical museum near harbour.

Brixham Cavern, Brixham, and *Kent's Cavern*, Babbacombe road, Torquay: limestone caves with stalagmite and stalactite features – a contrast to the surface limestone scenery of the coast.

Paignton: shopping; entertainment; Compton Castle (National Trust) near Paignton off Torbay ring road just north of Marldon; zoo and botanical gardens on Totnes road.

Torbay: aircraft museum west of Paignton; Aqualand aquarium, Torquay harbour.

Torquay: shopping; entertainment; beaches; Torre Abbey, promenade; Cockington Forge, near seafront (restored ford and mill).

Totnes: shopping; castle at head of main street; Dart Valley Railway, 7 miles (11 km) of track from Buckfastleigh, 2-hour return journey via Totnes (but no stop at Totnes); Guildhall, along the city wall.

Within reach of Plymouth

Dartmouth: shopping; castle (1 mile (1.6 km) west of town); Newcomen Engine House, Royal Avenue Gardens.

Plymouth: Drake's Island in Plymouth Sound (caves, fort, museum), boat from Mayflower Steps on the Barbican; Prysten House (15th century) behind St Andrew's Church; Saltram House (Tudor manor house and gardens), Royal Parade, 3 miles (5 km) east of Plymouth off A38; Buckland Abbey (National Trust), 8 miles north of Plymouth off A386 at Yelverton; Burrator Reservoir and forest trails near Yelverton; Dartmoor Wildlife Park, Sparkwell (25 acres of estate), east of Plymouth to Plympton then 3 miles east towards Cornwood; Devonshire Horse Farm Centre, Yealmpton, on Kingsbridge road out of Plymouth.

Slapton Ley: nature reserve; details of nature walks from Slapton Field Centre at village.

Tourist information centres

Brixham: Theatre. Tel. 2861
Exeter: Civic centre. Tel. 72434
Paignton: Festival Hall. Tel. 558387
Plymouth: Civic centre. Tel. 26485
Torquay: Vaughan Parade, near harbour. Tel. 27428

Information about the national park can be obtained from:

The Information Officer,
Dartmoor National Park Department,
Parke, Haytor Road,
Bovey Tracey, Devon, TQ13 9JQ

The National Park also operates several mobile information offices at popular places such as Postbridge and New Bridge. Look out for their portakabins in nearby car parks during the summer season.